The Real Candleford Green

The Story of a Lark Rise Village

Martin Greenwood

Nov-12th 1917 Stroud Bringford

My dear Florence you will thinks one a long time answering your long letter thanks very much for telling one such a lot of news I hope I shall soon get another one, and I hope that my Brother Henry is better and will enjoy many more years Please remember one to all and thanks to very much for the [?] I enjoy looking at them you have some wonderful things over there the

I shall be a body at last I am glad to tell you that my son is demobilised at last he was so glad to get home to his wife & child again but he has not got any work yet but we must look on hopes that he will soon have some. will you ask your one other if she thinks it will be safe to send your Brothers ring. I should thinks it would. poor soul it will upset her again to see it. but you must tell one what to do: give my love to them all and my love to you from your old Aunt Sarah Rennison

(Sarah Butler)

First page

Last page

Letter from Sarah Butler Rennison to Florence Rhoda Butler, daughter of her brother, Thomas, 12 November 1919. (Rhonda Smith).

future of the Aunt Hilda
are very interesting I have
shown them to several people
we are having some very
cold weather sharp frost
but dry tell your father
that Siebel's pond is frozen
over but of course not safe
the winter is beginning early
and I expect you are having
it nice and warm it
will soon be Christmas
I was hoping you would
get this by then but I
am afraid not I am sending
you a little keepsake
just in memory of me
the beads are too smart

for one to wear but you
must be sure to thread
them again as the string
has broke several times
and the ring is getting
too small for one and
besides I wanted to send
you something: forever
too much jewelery in
my young day and now
I am gettin too old: but
I have made myself a
black necklace I wear it
when I am dressed up
in the summer; and I shall
be 70 next April. and
that is a tidy of all of
us having 10/= a week's

Fringford Sunday Evening
6/2/98

My Dear Children
                        I was very glad to see a letter from
you yesterday and to hear you were all well
I said I should write last Sunday if I got a line if only P.C. before
but as I didnt get one I didnt write but am going to do
so now. all being well. not that I had anything in
particular to tell you as I know its no use for me
to tell you of my little petty troubles as I have —
you have enough to do to look after your little family
one thing I wanted to consult you about was a porch
at the front door before the winter came on but as
Rogers would not do it as I wanted I put it off by saying
I should consult you about it but as it is gone on so
far I shall leave it altogether during his lifetime as
poor old man it may not be long or it might be of
some months duration he has not been out since
before Xmas I have spent my Sundays most of them since
then with him his Sister has knocked herself up in doing
what she could for him so that she cant get out of doors
I must now tell you about our various alterations
in Fringford we are quite busy people about here/ as
to ourselves we have been very busy and I begun —
to think I shouldnt get any one in Wills place till
this last week I have had only one answer and one only to 6 weeks
advertisement and from his correspondence I think
he will suit us very well (he his coming to morrow
there are about 50 people Workmen of all classes down
at the Manor house (Mr Simons old house) and as
soon as the weather or I may say the days a little
longer Mr Millington told me the other day he should
be setting more hands on then the new stables
belonging are occupied by 2 Gentlemen visiting the

Letter from Kezia Whitton to her son, George, written just 5 days before she died,
6 February, 1898. (Whitton Family)

Gentleman at Cotmore I think there is 8 or 10 horses and
4 or 5 men it does seem funny to see Gentlemens horses
clothed up to and from from Manor house they are making
a new coach road round to the front towards Mr Paxton by
the churchyard Wall and think of putting a lodge again
the Swing gate and at the least 2 more cottages ———
they have already built a new bridge down again
Fridays Meadow (where that little narrow one was) to drive
out from it by the Morrell to this new station at Barley
Fields but whether it will be a Public road or not is a matter
of course after time I dont know — I was glad to hear when
you thought of coming up home but how many have
you thought of bringing with you and if you all think
of coming up during the next Summer as I should like
to know what your Ideas are about it as you must
remember that I have no spare bedroom now and shall
have to double them up together some way to get one bed and
more if I wanted more or send out but you will of course
know I cant have all of you at one time now especially
at the present time but after a bit I suppose Albert will
be getting married and that has been one of my petty troubles about
providing my house with meat for 3 men and then when that takes
place of course he will be wanting board wages which I know
you wont agree to my doing but you or rather I must keep those that
will stop and that you can rely upon as that has been one of my
troubles this winter the more people I have about me the more
difficult it is to get them to agree as C Knibbs and Sarah cant
agree no better than Will and Albert could agree in the shop ———
I have not seen anything of Fritwell people since before I was so had
not heard Loo was married — Fred is rather in a straitened
predicament (by what little he has told me which is not much) about his
Mother he says he cant see her go to the Workhouse so what is up I dont know
From Your Affectionate Mother

Note: the reference is to
Sarah 'Rennison'

Flora Thompson (née Timms), c1903, possibly when she married John Thompson. (Mickey Dunn)

The Real Candleford Green

The Story of a Lark Rise Village

Martin Greenwood

Published by
Robert Boyd Publications
260 Colwell Drive, Witney
Oxfordshire OX28 5LW

ISBN: 978 1 908738 22 6

First published 2016

© Martin Greenwood

Printed in the United Kingdom
by Henry Ling Limited
at the Dorset Press
Dorchester DT1 1HD

Contents

Front cover: Albert 'Noah' Price with his pony and trap in St. Michael's Close. Rosalind Marsh is on the pony. Others include: Tina Jones, Nick Wise, Neil Wickens and Carol Bond, taken in the 1970s. (Susan Gahan)

Back cover: The Old Forge, Fringford (Candleford Green), where Flora Thompson worked in the post office in the 1890s, painted by Julie Barrett, 2006. (Julie Barrett)

Pages 2 and 3: Letter from Sarah Butler Rennison to Florence Rhoda Butler, daughter of her brother, Thomas, 12 November 1919.

Pages 4 and 5: Letter from Kezia Whitton to her son, George, written just 5 days before she died, 6 February, 1898.

Tables

Illustrations

Colour photographs and illustrations

Foreword and Acknowledgements

In 2000 I published a millennium history of Fringford, entitled *Fringford Through the Ages*. Since then, BBC's Television adaptation of Flora Thompson's *Lark Rise to Candleford* (2008-10) has raised the profile of Fringford (*Candleford Green*) enormously. It has brought waves of new visitors to the village and led to the publication of a number of new books about Flora Thompson (1876-1947) and the Lark Rise villages. It has also led to contact with members of several old Fringford families, who have been happy to share their memories with me. In particular, I have been in touch with members of the Price family, who used to live at Pringle Cottage. They were plumbers, painters, and glaziers for about a century from 1852. By a stroke of good fortune, some of their business ledgers were found in the rafters of Pringle Cottage and passed on to me. Such records of a small village business are a rare find and it has been a pleasure to examine them in detail.

I have also been fortunate to be given a copy of a previously unpublished letter written by Flora Thompson in 1944, in which she outlines the extent to which *Lark Rise to Candleford* is autobiographical. I have also had access to some letters written by Kezia Whitton (Dorcas Lane in *Lark Rise),* and to some written by Sarah Butler Rennison, who was a letter-carrier immediately after Flora. Kezia's letters are written to her son, George, and shed some interesting light on her life in Fringford in the 1890s. Sarah was writing to her brother, Thomas, who had emigrated to Australia, along with three of his brothers. These letters reveal interesting details of her life as a letter carrier, and her relationship with her brothers in Australia. Research by Australian members of the Butler family tell us much about emigration in the 1870s and the fortunes of her brothers in North Queensland. These new discoveries and my own further research have yielded significant fresh information about the village, and inspired me to update the story of the Real Candleford Green.

In Chapter 1, I look at Flora Thompson's association with the village, and examine the extent to which her portrayal of *Candleford Green* is a true picture of nineteenth-century Fringford. I also look at the picture presented in the BBC TV series, which has done so much to raise the profile of the village. In Chapter 2, I look at the early years of Fringford, including a brief history of the manors and the Shelswell Estate, which has been an integral part of the life of the village for centuries. In Chapter 3, I take a stroll round the village, looking at the main buildings and their past occupants. In Chapter 4, I look at the village farms and the changes and decline in the number of active farms since 1850. In Chapter 5, I look at the history of Fringford church and its clergy. In Chapter 6, I look at Fringford's schools and education. In

Chapter 7, I look at some of the major changes in village life since the 1850s, including emigration, with a particular focus on the members of the Butler family who emigrated to Australia. In Chapter 8, I take a detailed look at the Price family from 1852 to 1953, and their surviving business ledgers. In Chapter 9, I look at the Roll of Honour, including those who died in the two World Wars and those who have been identified as fighting in the Great War and returning.

I am very grateful to all those who have helped me in my research for this book. In particular, I would like to thank Gladys Hinks, who has lived in the village for over 90 years and has been a wonderful source of information and link with the past. I would like to thank Bill Plumb for information about the Old Forge and his family's connections with it, and for use of some of his old photographs. I am grateful to David Taylor for information about the local farms and to Diana Joslin (née Taylor) for information and photographs of Cotmore. I am indebted to other past and present residents of Fringford, including Charles and Jinkie Hebditch, Kathleen Hunt (née Wyatt), Sheila Johnson, Judy Legg (née Standen), Norah Morgan, Dorothy Sparrow, and John and Mark Wyatt. My thanks to Baroness Anne von Maltzahn for information on the Shelswell estate and use of some of her photographs. I am grateful to Kevin Tobin for sharing his research on the Roll of Honour, and to Linda Mustill for her valuable assistance with researching village archives. I am indebted to Christine Bloxham for her invaluable books on the world of Flora Thompson, and to David Watts for sharing his treasure trove of photographs.

I would like to thank Jenni Pearse (née Price) and David Price for their information, memories and photographs of the Price family, and for permission to retain the Price ledgers for my research. Particular thanks also to Frideswide Curry for a copy of the letter from Flora Thompson to her aunt, Miss Eagle. I would like to thank the Whitton family for access to letters written by Kezia Whitton and other information about the family, Martin Mills for permission to quote from his Memories of Fringford School, and Peter Morrall for his photographs and information about the Mansfield family. I am grateful to Margaret Wilson for information about the de Salis family. I would also like to offer a special thank you to Joan Goodin and Grace Rutherford, who are sadly no longer with us, and to Rhonda Smith and Pat Spence, who have all shared their memories, photographs and research into the Butler family in North Queensland, Australia. I must also thank another member of the Butler family, Elizabeth Bagley of Idaho, USA, for letters, information and a photograph of Sarah Butler Rennison.

I would like to thank the staff at the Oxford History Centre (OHC) for their patience and assistance in answering my queries and allowing me to use some photographs from the collections of the Oxfordshire County Council Photographic Archive (OCC). I would also like to thank the staff at the Northamptonshire Record Office (NRO) and the National Archives for their assistance. I am extremely grateful to the Trustees of the Greening Lamborn Trust for their generous grant towards the cost of reproducing the illustrations. The Trust's objective is to promote public interest in the history, architecture, old photographs and heraldry of Oxford and its neighbourhood by supporting publications and other media that creates access to them.

I am very grateful to Peter Silver for his photographs and his skilled assistance in scanning and assembling all the photographs for publication. I am also grateful to Julie Barrett for her maps and beautiful paintings, and to the late Gordon Allen for access to the glass-plate photographs taken by his father, Thomas Henry Allen, in the 1920s and 1930s.

I am hugely indebted to Bob Boyd for all his assistance and advice in publishing this book. I would also like to offer a special thank you to Marilyn Yurdan for her rigorous but kindly reading of the text; her suggestions led to significant improvements in the text and presentation. I would also like to record my gratitude to the late James Nash for his gentle and helpful assistance with my two previous books. I shall always treasure my discussions with him and he is sorely missed after his untimely death. I would also like to record a more general thank you to Fringford and its residents past and present for their assistance with my researches and for making the past twenty-five years a very happy home for my wife, Anne, and myself. Finally, a very special thank you to Anne for her infinite patience while I have been writing and researching this book.

Martin Greenwood
Fringford, November 2015

CHAPTER 1

Candleford Green

'Candleford Green was taking its afternoon nap when they arrived. The large irregular square of turf which gave the village its name was deserted but for one grazing donkey and a flock of geese which came cackling with outstretched necks towards the spring-cart to investigate.'

'On the farther, less-populated side of the green a white horse stood under a tree outside the smithy waiting its turn to be shod, and, from within, as the spring-cart drew up, the ring of the anvil and the roar of the bellows could be heard.'[1]

This was the scene in 1891 when the fourteen-year-old Flora Timms (Laura) arrived in Candleford Green to work at the sub-post office with Kezia Whitton (Dorcas Lane). Some 60 years later, after the Second World War, the scene would have been very similar. 'Noah' Price's pony and Jim Wyatt's cows might have been grazing on the Green and the children were still going to the Old School. There was little change round the Green after the village hall was built in 1900, until the council houses were built there in the 1950s and the new school in 1973. As in 1891, many of the men would have been working in the fields, on the Shelswell Estate or in their workshops. Others had found work outside the village, for example, on the Upper Heyford Air Base, the Bicester Ordnance Depot, the Calvert Brick Works or Morris Motors at Cowley. Outside the forge a horse and cart and some farm machinery would probably have been waiting for the attention of Ernie Perrin. There might also have been a car or two awaiting William Plumb's magic touch. In his spare time from Morris Motors, he would repair cars and other engines, including his old Bullnose Morris (bought from William Grantham for 90 shillings!).

Fringford in the nineteenth century is now forever associated with Flora Thompson's *Lark Rise to Candleford*. It was originally published by Oxford University Press (OUP) as three separate books: *Lark Rise* (1939), *Over to Candleford Green* (1941), and *Candleford Green* (1943), and as a trilogy in 1945. In the books Laura (representing Flora herself) recalls her childhood in the hamlet of *Lark Rise* (Juniper Hill) and at school in *Fordlow* (Cottisford) before moving to *Candleford Green* (Fringford), where she worked in the sub-post office from 1891 to 1897. It is a vivid picture of village life at the end of the nineteenth century, and, uniquely, it was written by 'a child of poverty', who was able to avoid any sense of bitterness against the squire and his class. In many respects, village life had changed very little in the decades before 1876, when Flora was born. Deference to those above you was the norm and

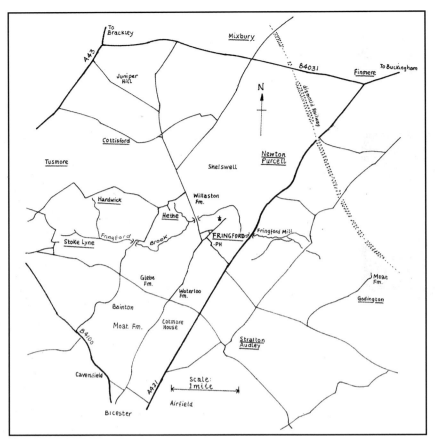

Map of Lark Rise Country. (Julie Barrett)

'Every member of the community knew his or her place and few wished to change it.'[2] It was a defining moment just before the agricultural depressions of the 1870s and 1890s and before the impact of major changes in health, housing and education.

It was most unusual for the OUP to publish such works, as they did not publish fiction. The initial run of 5,000 copies of the *Lark Rise* trilogy in 1945 was sold prior to publication. The book also received a magnificent testimonial from Sir Humphrey Milford, the publisher, who wrote that he considered the two most important books he had published during his twenty-two years at the Press were Arnold Toynbee's *A Study of History* and Flora Thompson's *Lark Rise to Candleford*. *Lark Rise* has been staged many times since the 1970s and it was made into a long-running BBC Television series from 2008 to 2010. This has contributed to a significant rise in the number of visitors to Fringford and what may now be called Lark Rise Country. In spite of Flora's fame, there had never been any memorial to her years in the village. Not before time, on 4 July 2010 at a special service in Fringford church, Linda Bassett (Queenie in the TV series) unveiled a plaque to commemorate Flora's years in the village (1891-97).

The Old Bake House, with Rose Cottage and Pringle Cottage, c.1910. (Bill Plumb)

The television series also raised further questions, not only about the accuracy of the TV version in relation to the book, but also about how faithful was Flora's own portrait of village life during her childhood. In an unpublished letter of 28 January 1944 (see below), Flora replied to a Miss Eagle, who must have asked her how strictly autobiographical the book was. Her reply sheds some light on her portrayal of *Lark Rise* and *Candleford Green*. She writes that 'Lark Rise is as far as I could make it a faithful portrait of the little Oxfordshire hamlet where I spent my childhood.' 'In Candleford and Candleford Green I wrote more freely, intending to give rather a picture of country life at that time and to portray some of the country characters I had known than to describe any particular town.' So there was some freedom in her portrait of Candleford Green, which emerges as rather more suburban with its villas and shops than it really was. She also admitted in the letter that 'there is something both of Banbury and Bicester and more of Buckingham in my picture of Candleford. It was actually to Buckingham we went in the spring-cart and some of my relatives lived there.' This in no way weakens her unique description of country life at the time.

In particular, the description of her life at the Post Office with Kezia Whitton rings true. She was to have a great influence on Flora, encouraging her to read a greater variety of books than she would have ever seen in Lark Rise. Little did she know how this experience would change her life and bring her fame as an author. Later she would write 'She was never to see any of these (landmarks) again, but she was to carry a mental picture of them, to be recalled at will, through the changing scenes of a lifetime.'[3] Some of the other characters at the Forge are based on known residents of Fringford: Matthew, the blacksmith, on Freddie Plumb, and Zillah, the servant,

The Old Bake House with Myrtle Wilkins (later Ayris) and the three Gough sisters crossing the Green in the 1940s. (Village Hall).

on Zilpha Hinks, both of them buried in Fringford churchyard. Zilpha was a general servant to the Whittons in 1881, but by 1891 she was a letter-carrier and living with her widowed mother, so there is some poetic licence in her portrayal as an older rather bad-tempered servant. In fact, she died in 1900 aged just 45.

Bill Gallagher, the writer and producer of the TV series, explained to a local audience some years ago, that it took him some ten years to bring *Lark Rise* to our screens. He has a passion for the book, which showed in the skill of the adaptation and the superb performances by many of the cast. One can open any page of the book and a wonderful character and story leap from it, which made it ideal for a series of episodes rather than a narrative approach. However, some confusion did arise about the relationship between the series and the original book, although the BBC made it clear that the series was 'based on the book'. The series started with Laura's move to Candleford, and the Forge and the Post Office were placed in the town rather than in the village of Candleford Green. Gallagher explained the thinking behind this decision. He saw Laura's move as a dramatic point when she enters the new world and new values of Candleford and leaves behind the old world and old values of Lark Rise. As Flora wrote of her move 'In the hamlet there lived only one class of people; all did similar work. All were poor and all equal. The

Lauriston,

Brixham, Devon.

January 28th 1944.

Dear Miss Eagle,

I am delighted to hear that you and your family enjoyed Lark Rise and the Candleford books. Many thanks for letting me know this.

Lark Rise is as far as I could make it a faithful portrait of the little Oxfordshire hamlet where I spent my childhood -- Juniper Hill, near Brackley. When Mr Lamb went there in 1939 to do the drawings which illustrate the book he found it little changed but I hear from more recent visitors that the war has had some effect upon it.

In Candleford and Candleford Green I wrote more freely, intending to give rather a picture of country life at that time and to portray some of the country characters I had known than to describe any particular town. There

(*continued over the page*)

Previously unpublished letter from Flora Thompson to Miss Eagle, 28 January 1944. This was found, after Miss Eagle's death in 2007, in her copy of *Lark Rise to Candleford*, by her niece, Frideswide Curry. Muriel 'Molly' Eagle (b. 1916) was a legendary teacher at St Mary and St John's Primary School in Oxford for 37 years.

is something both of Banbury and Bicester
and more of Buckingham in my picture of
Candleford. It was actually to Buckingham
we went in the spring cart and some of my
relatives lived there. I hope you will not
be disapppinted to find Candleford still
somewhat elusive. With many thanks for
your interest in the places,
              yours very sincerely,
                              Flora Thompson

population of Candleford Green were more varied.'[4] It must also be said that, by moving the Forge to a town, it provided a greater variety of storylines, including a boutique, a journalist and a hotel.

Laura was overjoyed when she was allowed to start delivering letters rather than just sorting them in the office. There was also an extra 'four shillings a week which was considered quite a substantial addition to incomes larger than Laura's in those days.'[5] This seems to have been in 1894, as she mentions that she did it for nearly three years, and she left Fringford in 1897. She joined Mrs Gubbins, an older lady, in doing the cross-country deliveries, which included Willaston, Shelswell and the estate cottages. 'Mrs Gubbins had got herself up to face the weather by tying a red knotted shawl over her head and wearing the bottom of a man's trouser-legs as gaiters.'[6]

By a happy coincidence, we know something of a later Fringford letter-carrier, Sarah Rennison (née Butler), who was born in Fringford in 1850. She is recorded as a dressmaker in the 1891 census, but by 1901 she is a letter-carrier, and in 1911 she is described as a rural postwoman. There is evidence that she was a letter-carrier at least by 1898 (see Chapter 7), so it seems more than likely that she replaced Flora. She would certainly have known her, as she was living only a few steps from the Forge, in her father's old house on Main Street (part of The Cottage). Four of her brothers emigrated to Australia (see Chapter 7) and a letter, which she wrote to her brother, Thomas, in Northern Queensland about 1916, has survived. It shows that she was still delivering letters during the First World War, when she must have been doing the same morning round as Laura and wrapping up like Mrs Gubbins to keep out the cold. 'They told me this morning that I looked like a red Indian in my big boots and gaiters and waterproof skirt and my red face.'[7]

By then she was well over sixty, and working for Ernest and Ellen Price at the Pringle Cottage post office. We do not know how long she continued to do the letter-round but she lived on in Fringford on her own until 1932. Only then, aged 82, did she reluctantly agree to join her son near Bristol, where she died the following year. We shall see more of Sarah in Chapters 3 and 7.

It is time now to look at the story of Fringford, the real Candleford Green, from its early years to the present day.

Chapter 1 footnotes

[1] Flora Thompson, *Lark Rise to Candleford*, 393 (Penguin 1973).

[2] *Lark Rise*, 417.

[3] *Lark Rise*, 537.

[4] *Lark Rise*, 416.

[5] *Lark Rise*, 509.

[6] *Lark Rise*, 504.

[7] Letter from Sarah Butler Rennison to her brother, Thomas Butler, in Queensland, c.1916.

Chapter 2

The Early Years

Fringford is an ancient site and seems to have been inhabited for most, if not all, of the past 2000 years. The name is thought to mean 'ford of the people of Fera', the Feringas, a Saxon tribe or family group, who were here well before the Norman Conquest. In 1993, an excavation at Crosslands in the centre of the village revealed a complex series of Romano-British and later features, with evidence of occupation from the late 2nd to the 4th century AD, and enclosure ditches of the 10th-11th- century date. Other work, at Fringford Lodge (on the Bicester road), produced evidence of a possible Romano-British villa with a hypocaust. In 1996, excavations at Fringford Manor provided evidence of significant remains of medieval date, including a medieval moated site with an associated boundary and fish pond. In the twelfth century, the site underwent a major change, possibly due to the establishment of the 'principal estate'. This was known to be in existence in 1288 and comprised a (manor) house and garden, with 120 acres of arable and 2 acres of meadow. This house almost certainly lay on or close to the site of Manor Farm.

In 1997, excavations in Farriers Close (formerly The Paddock) revealed evidence of medieval occupation in the form of 11/12th-century enclosures and field boundaries, and 13th-century stone buildings and associated yards, ditches and pits. Evidence was also revealed of Romano-British field boundaries relating to a possible settlement to the north-east. The most unusual discovery was a Romano-British cremation burial with a large number of iron nails. It is likely that the individual had been wearing hobnailed boots and was placed in a wooden coffin before being burnt on a cremation pyre. There are few other known examples from Oxfordshire of such a cremation burial with footwear. In the second half of the thirteenth century, three stone buildings were constructed, one of which appears to have been a farrier's workshop. The buildings may have formed part of a manorial complex before they were apparently abandoned in the fourteenth century. This was the period of the Black Death and other plagues, which led to large-scale depopulation and the disappearance of settlements like Tusmore.[8]

Fringford lies in a loop of the Bure, a tributary of the river Ouse, with Fringford bridge on the north-west and the old corn mill and Fringford Mill bridge to the east. If one stood by Fringford bridge in December 2013 and looked at the flooded fields, with Fringford safe on the hill above, one could see why the Feringas must have felt secure there. Blomfield, writing in 1890, noted that once a road (now Rectory Lane)

Shelswell Park, with the stable block on the right, 1901. (OCC)

ran from the village green straight across the field on the west side of the Rectory down to the stream, where a stone-paved way went to Willaston, Shelswell and Mixbury. He also noted that traces of a second ford were still visible on the west side of the bridge, which was used after the hamlets of Willaston and Shelswell became depopulated in the sixteenth century and its traffic diverted to Hethe and Cottisford[9]. Sheep pasture became more economic than arable land and so it was said 'sheep ate up men'.[10] By 1601 enclosure [of some 500 acres] was said to be complete and, to make the enclosure more effectual, the old village was destroyed soon afterwards.[11] The older ford then fell into disuse, and the road from the village was diverted across Bancroft to Fringford Bridge. Within living memory, the rector used to drive this way from the Rectory to Hethe to take church services. About 1840 the present bridge replaced a narrow single-arch bridge, of which some traces remain.

Fringford Manors
The first documentary reference to the village of Fringford occurs in the Domesday Book (1086), which describes the village as containing two estates, with some 30 villagers. The 1279 Hundred Rolls list the names of a similar number. The Taxation Records of 1316 list 31 property-holders, although these taxpayers almost certainly

do not represent the total number of households. By 1525 the number of property-holders had shrunk to 25, although the average size of holding of these men had risen considerably. From an early date Fringford manor was divided into two ' moieties', i.e. halves, the North and South Manors. As we have seen, in 1288 the principal estate was near the site of Manor Farm. At the same time, the South Manor 'which belonged to the Lords de Grey consisted of Cotmore, and the parts most distant from the village on its west side.'[12] However, it was no more than a few scattered cottages until the early nineteenth century. The manor house was probably on the site of Moat Farm (formerly Cotmore Farm). The manor passed to the Greville family in the sixteenth century and by the time of the Enclosure Award of 1762 Sir Fulke Greville was the chief owner of the whole manor. The North Manor consisted of the village and land nearest to it. In the sixteenth century this passed to the Wenmans, who were great merchants and clothiers at Witney. They built a new manor house close to the site of the Old School. However, by the time of the Enclosure Award both manor houses had disappeared.

Enclosure

In the seventeenth century the various Hearth Tax returns and the Compton Census of 1676 indicate that Fringford had some 30 houses and a population of around 130. During the eighteenth century the village grew and by 1801 there were about 50 houses and a population of 252. By the time of the Enclosure Award, as has been noted, some 500 acres had already been enclosed by the Lords of Shelswell Manor. The Award effectively meant the end of the open field system with its medieval style of strip-farming. Under the Award, Sir Fulke Greville received 385 acres, while the other principal beneficiaries were the rector, the Revd John Russell Greenhill (227 acres), Anthony Addington of Hall Farm (89 acres) and Eton College (71 acres), which also owned most of Cottisford. The College's main holdings in Fringford were around the Mill and Church Farm (Appendix 1). It sold off its remaining holdings in Fringford and Cottisford in 1920-21.

Shelswell Manor

Shortly after its Enclosure, the North Manor's lands were sold to Lord Holland, who in turn in 1815 sold them to John Harrison. In 1782, his father, Gilbert Harrison, had bought the neighbouring Shelswell Manor from the Trotman family, and the manor with its large estate has dominated the surrounding area, including Fringford, for centuries. In 1844, it was reported that 'Nearly if not the whole of Fringford is the property of JHS Harrison Esq.'[13] The Tithe Award of 1848 shows that he owned 50 of the 83 properties listed (Appendix 1). In 1873, the 'Modern Domesday Survey' of landowners recorded JHS Harrison of Shelswell Park as owning some 4,716 acres. This was significantly more than his neighbours, Sir Thomas Peyton at Swift's House in Stoke Lyne with 1,977 acres, and the Earl of Effingham at Tusmore Park with 3,376 acres.

Left: Edward Slater-Harrison, in hunting dress, 1903. (OCC). Right: John Dewar-Harrison (mounted) talking to Lord Chesham at a Meet of the Bicester Hounds at Fringford Bridge in 1923/24. (Baroness von Maltzahn)

In 1875, Edward Slater-Harrison pulled down the old Trotman manor and built a new mansion, designed by the Oxford architect William Wilkinson. He also enlarged the park and added plantations. It was here that Flora Thompson went in the summer of 1891 to sign on with 'Sir Timothy', as she refers to him. 'She sensed the atmosphere of jollity, good sense, and good nature, together with the smell of tobacco, stables, and country tweeds he carried around like an aura.'[14] Edward died in 1911 but his second wife, Emma Cecilia (née Cartwright), continued to live here until her death in 1943.

Edward had no son and was succeeded by his nephew, Major Arthur William Dewar, on condition that he added the name 'Harrison' to his own. At that time he was living in Hethe House, which may have been built as a Dower House by the Trotmans. He moved to the farmhouse at Willaston, where he died in 1923. This second death within 12 years meant a heavy incidence of death duties on the family and the estate. Arthur was succeeded by his eldest son, John Francis Dewar-Harrison, who was squire for 44 years until his death in 1967. He continued to live

The Funeral Cortege of John Dewar-Harrison, 1967. (Baroness von Maltzahn)

at Willaston, while Emma Cecilia stayed on at Shelswell House, where she was said to have maintained it 'in its ancient glory, with beautiful gardens, greenhouses, fishponds, watercress beds and a plant house with a thousand plants. She kept six full time gardeners and six housemaids, all of whom remember her for her motherly care, and was guarded by six fierce dogs.'[15] The two world wars had a major effect on many of the large country houses and Shelswell had given up most of its ancient glory, including most of its gardeners and other staff, by the time she died.

During the Second World War, the fields opposite Middle Farm were made into an airfield, where the hedgerows were removed and replaced with irregular cinder tracks, which looked like hedges from the air. A maintenance unit was based there. Featherbed Lane was closed to traffic as bombs were stored there, the park had various nissen huts built under the trees and Shelswell House was used to house RAF officers. After the war the house was converted into flats for local families. By the late 1970s it had become almost uninhabitable and it was demolished in the early 1980s. The surviving stable block was gutted by fire in 1983 but a major refurbishment was completed in 2000 and it is now rented as a private dwelling .

On the death of John Dewar-Harrison in 1967, one of his closest friends was quoted as saying 'He was the last of the Squires and Country Gentleman.'[16] He was certainly very popular in Fringford and the surrounding villages. The house and land had to be sold and several of the farms were bequeathed to his tenant farmers in return for payment of their share of the estate duty. As he never married, the residue of his estate passed to his goddaughter, Lydia Anne Smith, later Baroness Anne von Maltzahn. She and the Baron, who have three children, continue to live at The Home Farm House in Shelswell.

Chapter 2 footnotes

8 OAU Occasional Paper No.6, 2000 is the basis for this paragraph.

9 J.C.Blomfield, *Deanery of Bicester, Part V. History of Fringford, Hethe, Mixbury, Newton Purcell, and Shelswell* (1890/91), *Fringford*, 8-9.

10 Sir Thomas More (1478-1535), *Utopia, Book 1, Pasturage destroying Husbandry* (1516).

11 Blomfield, *Shelswell*, 10.

12 Blomfield. *Fringford*. 14.

13 *Oxford Chronicle*, 16 November.1844.

14 *Lark Rise*, 415.

15 John M.Sergeant, *The Story of Hethe*, 15 (1980s).

16 *Bicester Advertiser*, 10 February 1967.

Chapter 3

A Stroll Round the Village

The influence of the Shelswell Estate on the village has already been mentioned. In the nineteenth century, the village was also dominated by a series of well-connected, wealthy rectors, who were prepared to make substantial contributions to the church and parish. In 1700, there were 34 houses and by 1801 there were some 50 houses and a population of 252. By 1851, there were 80 houses and a population of 357. It reached its peak of 479 in 1871, but by 1901 it had fallen to 335 with 94 houses. In 1951, there were still only 331 inhabitants. Since the Second World War, following a number of housing developments, the population has nearly doubled and in 2011 there were 249 houses with a population of 602. Initial housing developments in the 1960s, in Church Close and St Michael's Close, were followed by those in Manor Road and later ones in Crosslands and Farriers Close. The village still has a primary school and a public house but no shops. As with other villages in the area, the population has been largely dependent on agriculture.

We begin our walk at the Butchers Arms by the Cricket Ground (GR 605286).

Stratton Audley Road
The BUTCHERS ARMS is seventeenth- and eighteenth-century and it was certainly licensed by 1735. In 1774, there was a Bricklayers Arms in the village – probably the same inn. James Hodgkins took over as publican from John Price about 1863. He was born in Priors Marston, Warwickshire, but his wife, Elizabeth, was born nearby in Hethe. He was the publican until his death in 1890 but he also 'multi-tasked' as a wheelwright and blacksmith. Later, Albert Green ran the pub from 1913 to 1955, and he also ran a taxi service. The pub, which is said to be haunted by the ghost of a 'Rose Brennan', who is said to have been murdered here, continues to flourish, providing a warm welcome and fine food.

The MALT HOUSE, behind the pub, dates from the eighteenth century or earlier. A doorway in the back room of the pub used to lead through to the Malt House. There used to be a smithy up Green Lane, the path on the north side.

The COUNCIL HOUSES in Wise Crescent opposite, and on the Stratton Audley Road beyond the pub, were built in the early 1950s. They had all the modern

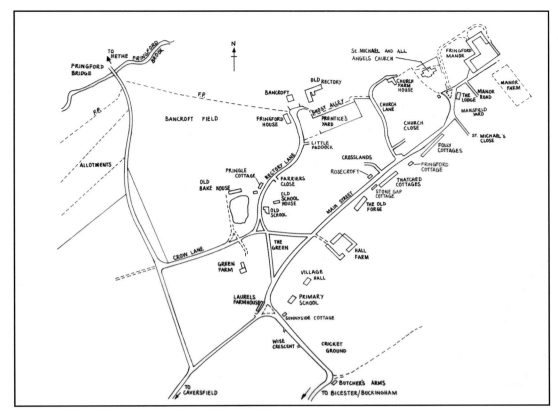

Map of Fringford. (Julie Barrett)

conveniences, which represented a major advance in the standard of housing in the village. Initially, weekly rents for the two-bedroomed type were 15s. inclusive of rates. By 1958, rents were 18s.with rates an extra 4s.11d., plus 1s.3d.for an electric cooker. In the 1990s, all the houses in the Stratton Audley Road were modernised and refaced. More recently, the houses have all been fitted with solar panels.

Walk past the cricket ground to the large chestnut tree by the Village Green. About 50 yards from the pub, where there is a slight hollow on the right, this used to be a small pool called 'Claydons Pond' on which the children would skate in the winter.

The CRICKET GROUND was leased to the Cricket Club in 1901 by Henry Chinnery. The Club celebrated its centenary in 2001, although in the 1890s the rector, the Revd Charles Thompson (Mr Delafield), is said to have put cricket 'upon a proper footing, with an eleven of young men and practice nights for boys'.[17] Interestingly, there is also a photograph of a women's eleven in 1915. In 2013, the Cricket Club purchased the ground from the trustees of the Chinnery family, with the aid of a grant from the English Cricket Board.

Mrs Omar's shop, on the left, with a view of the Butchers Arms. Note her Morris 8 and the sign for Eldorado ice cream, 1950s. (Sue Gahan).

Stratton Audley Road, with the new council houses and the water tower, early 1950s. (Sue Gahan)

Fringford Ladies Cricket XI, postcard c.1915. Agnes Plumb, daughter of Frederick Plumb, is sitting in the front row on the right. (Bill Plumb).

PAVILION VIEW, the first house on the right, has been built very recently.

SUNNYSIDE COTTAGE: Amy Claydon ran a shop here in the 1920s and Mrs Tye took it over from her. After the Second World War, it was the home of Phyllis and Arthur Omar. Phyllis, whose sister Ivy ran the pub in neighbouring Hethe, ran the shop here for many years before Jack Wise bought it. His brother Dick Wise took it over and let his daughter, Sue Gahan, run it with help from her sister, Ann Blake. Bill and Sue Jones took it on for the last few years before it closed in the late 1970s. The cottage was rebuilt in the 1980s.

SUNNYSIDE HOUSE, next door, was the site of a smithy, where Albert Jackman worked until his death in 1951. Ernest Perrin bought it in 1953 when he left the Old Forge, and he ran it with his brother. When it closed in the 1960s, Jack Wise bought the building and used it as a storeroom.

Turn right by the large chestnut tree to admire the classic Village Green.

The Green
The typical setting of a medieval village grouped round the Green survives. The old farmhouses, Laurels Farmhouse and Green Farm on the left and Hall Farm beyond the Village Hall, all date from the seventeenth century or earlier. In the sixteenth century, there was also a manor on the far side of the Green, on the site of the Old

School. After Enclosure in 1762, new farms like Waterloo Farm and Glebe Farm were built outside the village. 'In a hollow at its north end is a large pound [by Hall Farm], near which may generally be seen a few representatives of the geese tribe, who through many long years have fed and quacked upon the greensward.'[18] Such geese were still alive and well during Flora Thompson's years in the village, and much later, when they lived on the Old Bake House pond and used to come to the Old School at lunch time to be fed.

LAURELS FARMHOUSE, formerly The Laurels, on the corner by the chestnut tree, is listed as late seventeenth or early eighteenth century. Parts, including some cellars and an old staircase, may be earlier. George Gibbard farmed here from the 1850s, and in 1883 he was described as brewer, farmer and maltster. After his death in 1894, his widow, Ann, farmed it with her son, Thomas. The Gibbards continued to farm here until Thomas died in 1938 and Albert Wise bought the farm (see also Chapter 4). There used to be an off-licence here and people would sit outside with their drinks. During the Second World War, they used the air-raid shelter, which had been dug in the garden.

THE LAURELS: these new houses, behind the farmhouse, were built when the farmland was sold in the 1980s. In the 1990s, Richard Wise sold Laurels Farm and built a new farmhouse, also called The Laurels, on the back road leading to Caversfield.

FRINGFORD CHURCH OF ENGLAND PRIMARY SCHOOL, on the right, was opened in 1973 to replace the Old School on the other side of the Green. The school continues to flourish with over 100 pupils on roll. In February 2003, the Playgroup also moved across the Green to a new building next to the school. The Playgroup site used to be known as 'Jackman's Garden', after Albert Jackman, the blacksmith of Sunnyside. In the early 1900s there was still an old cottage here, with two large willow trees in the garden.

The VILLAGE HALL was built by Henry Chinnery on land given by the local squire, Edward Slater-Harrison. It was formally opened by Mr Chinnery in June 1900 and presented to the village as a reading-room for the men of the village and a place for meetings and entertainments. In 1901, it was described in the local press as 'the new parish room', where 'there would be parish meetings, mothers meetings, guild meetings, concerts and sing-songs', in short everything that would tend to the improvement of the people of the village. Tea and entertainment were provided on New Year's Day. The entertainment included singing, recitations, and a cinemato-graph exhibition by Mr Timms of Oxford.[19] The Chinnery Room and the kitchens were added in 1968. The Chinnery Room has just been rebuilt, and the whole hall has been substantially modernised and refurbished.

The Cottage on the Green, before it was rebuilt by Roy Ayris, 1950s. (Judy Legg)

Walk across the Green past Laurels Farmhouse

GREEN FARM / GREEN FARM COTTAGE: The farm is listed as late seventeenth century and part of an old newel staircase may date from this period. There are also eighteenth-century additions. Parts, including an old floor, may be earlier. The Domesday Valuation of 1910 (Appendix 2) records Mrs Ann and Thomas Gibbard, her son, as tenants of Edward Slater-Harrison, farming some 62 acres. By the late 1930s the building had been subdivided and the Wilkins and Hancocks were living here; Walter Wilkins farmed the land, while Hubert 'Bert' Hancock took over the bakery at the Old Bake House. In 1959/60 the Wilkins moved out and Roy Tew moved from his farm in Godington into the main house, where he continued to live with his housekeeper until the early 1980s. He then moved into Green Farm Cottage, the two-storey building on the west end, where he stayed until his death in the early 1990s. The eighteenth-century barn to the rear has been converted into a private dwelling, Meadow Barn.

CROW LANE was the old name for the lane leading to the Hethe road, as there used to be elm trees on both sides, full of crows. There were gardens on the west side, some of them used by the children from the Old School for growing vegetables.

ALLOTMENTS, known as the 'Bridge Ground' allotments, used to be on the left of the Hethe road before Fringford Bridge. An 1899 plan of them, with a schedule of

The Old Bake House, with baker's carts, c.1910. (Peter Crook).

allotment rentals, survives. There were 65 allotments of varying sizes, with rentals from 2s.1d. (10.45p) to 5s.3d.(26.3p) per half-year, payable on Lady Day and Michaelmas. There were also some allotments known as 'Crabdy (or Crabtree) Piece' on the right of the back road near Waterloo Farm. They were all given up in the 1950s.

THE COTTAGE, on the corner of Crow Lane, was sold by John Dewar-Harrison to Roy and Myrtle Ayris in the late 1950s. It was said to have been sold 'for a song and a handshake' like a number of other properties in the village. It was a seventeenth- or early eighteenth-century thatched cottage, which Roy, with much local help, rebuilt almost completely. Lena Knibbs, who was a member of the Ladies Cricket X1 in 1915, was still living here in the 1940s.

THE OLD BAKE HOUSE dates from the seventeenth century. By 1851, William Sirett (aged 32) and his wife, Ann (30), were running the bakery. Ann continued to run it after William's death in 1876. By 1891, her son, Ebenezer, had taken it over, although she was still living there, aged 72, and was no doubt still involved. By 1901, William Henry Biggers had succeeded them and also taken over the Post Office from John and Mary Wyatt (see Chapter 7). By 1910, he had returned to Eynsham, where he was born, to take over the Swan Public House, and Ernest and Ellen Price at Pringle Cottage on Rectory Lane had taken over the Post Office. At the same time, James Harold Crook moved here from Waddesdon, where he was born, with his wife, Mary Jane, and his children, Agnes (4), Ellis Charles (2) and Ruth Ellen (1). He also had a servant, Annie Timmes [sic] (aged 16). He was related to William Biggers on his mother's side. He used to wear a cape and a big black hat, which scared the children. The Field Books of 1913-15 describe the Bakehouse as follows:

'Bakery, 1 acre and 35 perches. A v.old stone & slated hse with bakery annexed cont'g Bakehouse with rough tiled floor & oven, 2 good sitting rms, tiled kitchen & larder on grd fl; 3 brms, bathroom & cupboard & flour room on 1st fl., in front is a small flower garden enclosed by iron fence, at RH side a veg gdn with wall behind a small paddock & orchard. Behind the bake-house is a wood & gal.iron large cart shed & 3 stall stable in poor repair; an old stone & slated cart shed with side way. The hse is in gd internal but poor structural repair. Right of way to water in favor of No.258 (Price) [Rose Cottage].'

Harold Crook lived in the Bakehouse until his death in 1963, although he handed over the bakery to Bert Hancock of Green Farm in the late 1930s. He was followed by Mr Newby and then Les Morgan. Les is remembered for the quality of his cakes and his distinguished record as a navigator in Lancaster bombers, although he never spoke about it. His surviving log-book shows that he flew 38 missions over Germany, including several of the massive bomber raids. He was awarded the Belgian Croix de Guerre with palm, for his contribution to the liberation of Belgium. The bakery closed in the late 1960s when he moved to Stratton Audley to run the post office. The Rawlinson family lived in the house from 1976 to 1986. By mutual agreement, they took over the pond from the parish council and cleaned it up. Since then Jane Burn and her family have lived there and she has undertaken major refurbishment to the house and garden. The pond is now surrounded by trees and nearly invisible from the Green, so that one would never guess that it was once the village pond.

THE OLD SCHOOL was built as a National (i.e. Church of England) School by the rector, Henry de Salis, on land leased from John Harrison Slater- Harrison. It opened in 1866 with places for 80 pupils. This was the site of the sixteenth-century North Manor, which, 'within living memory in the late nineteenth century, retained distinct traces of a gentleman's residence, a broad staircase leading to a large upper room on the second floor and several bed-chambers, with large cellars below. Subsequently this house fell into bad repair, and in the early 1800s was used as a parish poor-house. Five families, and sometimes more, who could find no other residences, were quartered here in its several rooms, and hence the house was known as "The Barracks". The large upper room was then long used as a Sunday Schoolroom, until the whole building was pulled down in or about 1830.'[20] In 1929, a fourth classroom

The Old School, before 'the Hut' was erected, 1920s. (OCC)

was added, allowing admission of children over 11 from Cottisford, Hethe, Newton Purcell and Stratton Audley. In 1931, a fifth classroom, 'the Hut', was erected at a cost of £125.

In 1949, Fringford was reorganised as a Junior Central School, and seniors now moved on to Bicester. In 1951, the managers handed the school over to the Local Education Authority (LEA). In 1973, the 'old school' was closed and the 'new school' opened on the other side of the Green. The old school became a Victorian Study Centre and in the early 1980s 'the Hut' became home to the Shelswell Playgroup. In 2003, the Playgroup relocated to a new building on the new school site. In 2004, the old school site was sold and the school building was converted to a private house. The developers commented at the time on the superior quality of the original stonework which probably came from the Cotswolds. Conversion included the demolition of 'the Hut' which had survived since 1931 (See Chapter 5 for further discussion of Schools and Education in the village).

THE OLD SCHOOL HOUSE next door was built in 1876 on land leased from Lord Sidmouth, the owner of Hall Farm. The 1910 Valuation Book records W.H.Robinson (head-teacher) occupying the 'Sch.mgrs house & garden'. He was assistant overseer, assessor and collector of taxes, and it was he who signed off the Fringford Valuation Book on 25th November, 1910 (Appendix 2). The head-teachers lived here until 1964 when the house was sold.

COTTAGES ON THE GREEN: Nos.1 and 2 were built about 1960, Nos.3 and 4 about 1950, and Nos.5 and 6 in 1929. Albert White used to live in Number 6, now called Willmand House. He always smoked a pipe, grew his own tobacco and hung

Albert Price with his pony and trap in St Michael's Close. Rosalind Marsh is on the pony. Others include: Tina Jones. Nick Wise, Neil Wickens and Carol Bond, 1970s. (Sue Gahan).

it out in the attic – the smell is still remembered! For many years Albert Price lived in Rose Cottage, an old thatched cottage on the site of No.1. Albert, known as 'Noah', was a legendary character in the village, and much loved by the children. He was a painter and decorator like others in the Price family. He rode an old motor bike with a sidecar in which he kept his ladder and all his decorating equipment. It was only on rare occasions that this equipment seems to have been used. He was a great talker and, as one builder used to say, 'Lock him in and keep him in'! Otherwise no work was done. When he was commissioned by Albert Green to redecorate the pub, he painted one room and then left without returning! Charles Freeman and his parents lived here before him. Charles carved the pew ends, the vestry wall and the choir stalls in the church (see below).

SPRING HOUSE, formerly Number 7 The Green, was built fairly recently on part of the garden of No.6, where there used to be a pump for use by those living on the Green.

HALL FARM, formerly Fringford Hall Farm, has been owned by the Addington family for some 400 years, although they have not lived here since 1746. Dr Anthony Addington (1713-90) was doctor to William Pitt the Elder (the Earl of Chatham) and to George III during his 'madness'. In 1788 he was the only doctor to successfully predict the king's recovery from what is now known to have been porphyria. His son, Henry (1757-1844), became Speaker and later Prime Minister (1801-4) and the first Lord Sidmouth. The farmhouse is listed as early seventeenth century with eighteenth- and twentieth-century alterations, and is essentially two buildings. Part of the north end may date from the fourteenth century. The two-storey addition on the south-west side was built in the late seventeenth century and a brick dovecote survives at the rear between the ground and first floors. The early seventeenth-century part contains a plaster carving of the royal coat of arms, which is likely to have been put up by the Addingtons. People were encouraged to put them up to demonstrate loyalty to the Hanoverian kings, particularly at the time of Bonnie Prince Charlie and the Jacobite Rebellion of 1745, that is just before the Addingtons left the village. There is also a Sun Assurance fire-mark above the back door. These fire-marks were proof of insurance to the Fire Brigade and also good company advertising. Early ones were made of lead and often had a policy number on them, as this one has. As it probably dates from the early eighteenth century, it would have been put up by the Addingtons.

In 1890, Blomfield commented that 'The house long occupied by the Addington family still stands on the village green, though sadly modernised and deprived of its former picturesque appearance.' At the same time Lord Sidmouth remembered a long current tradition that one of his ancestors was said to be frequently seen riding on a white horse in the cellars of the house where the Addington ale, famous for its potency, was stored.'[21] For much of the nineteenth century and the first half of the twentieth century the Mansfield family farmed here (see Chapter 4). The Field Books 1913-15 record George Mansfield, as tenant of Viscount Sidmouth, with 122 acres but 'The hse is old & in poor condition & the bldgs immediately behind same are in v.moderate condition.' Lovell Buckingham took over the farm from the Mansfields in the late 1930s and farmed it with his sons until Ian Thomas took over the tenancy in March 1965. His son, Charlie, now runs the farm and 'Fringford Feeds, Horse, Pet and Poultry Supplies'.

Main Street
THE FORGE is listed as mid-eighteenth century with twentieth century alterations, although there is evidence that the building may have been constructed c.1597. It also used to be the sub-post office, where Flora Thompson (née Timms) worked as assistant post-mistress from 1891 to 1897. In her time the forge and the post office were run by Kezia Whitton (Dorcas Lane in *Lark Rise*); her husband, John, had died shortly after Flora's arrival. Kezia Kirby, daughter of a blacksmith, had married John Whitton in 1857 and they moved from Stoke Lyne to Fringford to run the forge. John did a variety of work for the church and the Whitton name is on the entrance gate to the churchyard. By 1883 the Whittons had also taken on the new Sub-Post Office, Money Order Office & Savings Bank.

Main Street in the 1920s, before the porches were added to the thatched cottages. Albert Price's motor bike and side-car are in the foreground. Gable Cottage (recently demolished) is on the right. (Gordon Allen)

They had four children who died at birth or shortly after in the years 1858-61, and only two survived infancy: George born in 1863 and Alexander born in 1866. Alexander died at the age of twenty-four, when working as an accountant on the Gold Coast. He is buried next to his parents in Fringford churchyard. George became a Customs and Excise Officer in Liverpool. The two boys went to the Free Grammar School at Courteenhall, near Northampton (Appendix 3). It says much about the ambitions of Kezia Whitton that she sent the boys away to a Grammar School, where they must have been boarders. This was a great age for private schools and many Victorian farmers and tradesmen were ambitious for their children to receive a better education.

Examination of the school registers reveals that George and Alexander were almost the only boys who were not local, apart from one from 'Barbadoes' and another from London who left as being 'too weakly to attend'. The registers also record the impressive curriculum provided for the boys (Appendix 3). George was at the school from 20 December 1875 to 9 November 1877, Alexander from 22 January 1878 to 2 May 1879. Before then, they were both at Fringford school, where the register records them among the first ten pupils at the new National School built in 1866. At the time, it was normal to leave school aged 12 and most of the Fringford pupils left then to go to work on the land. It is interesting that Frederick Mansfield, who had also been at Fringford school, joined Alexander at Courteenhall from 22 January 1878 to 15 August 1879. He was a son of John and Mary Mansfield, who ran a grocer's shop in Mansfield Yard (see below).

Kezia and John were both very large; Kezia weighed over 18 stone and John over 22 stone. John died on 23 August 1891, aged 61, just after Flora must have arrived. She has left a colourful picture of Kezia: 'Had she lived a century earlier or half a century later, she would probably have been found at the forge with a sledge-hammer in her hand for she had an indomitable energy and a passion for doing and making things'[22]. Kezia's surviving letters show how involved and interested she was in everything going on in the village, but sadly none of them make any mention of Flora. Her comments on 6 February 1898, just five days before she died, show how she still wanted to improve the building: 'one thing I wanted to consult you about was a porch at the front door before the winter came on- but Rogers [the village carpenter] would not do it as I wanted - I put it off by saying that I wanted to consult you about it.'[23] The porch was put on later by Frederick Plumb, her foreman blacksmith (Matthew in *Lark Rise*). After Kezia's death, it was he who had to take out the left hand upstairs bedroom window, so that her coffin could be lowered down a ladder; it was too large to carry down the narrow stairs. One can still see where he subsequently patched up the window with bricks.

Earlier, on 9 September 1897, Kezia had some comments on the postal work: 'I don't know what alteration they are going to make in postal work again- I am sure there has been a Surveyor down at Bicester for a fortnight inspecting every mans route and every house is to have a delivery and they do say every office is to be made a telegraph office (if so I shall have to give up.). I cant learn that- and I spoke to Fred one day something respecting it and he says I wont advise you or have anything to do with your post office, for I would throw it out in the Street.' This tells us something about the bureaucracy in the post office (nothing changes) and Fred's strong views on it. Kezia clearly relied on Fred and in the same letter, she writes of her need for money (reason not given): 'I have asked Fred if he would lend me £30 or 40- by paying the same interest as he gets from the P.O.S.B.[Post Office Savings Bank] and he says he will.' Otherwise 'dont you think that Mr Tubb [the Bicester banker] would lend me the loan of 40 or 50, as there will be interest as well as the principal to be paid.'

After Kezia's death, George Whitton owned the Forge, while Frederick Plumb took over the tenancy. At the same time, John and Mary Wyatt, who were recently married and living in an old cottage on the site of Rosemary Cottage, took over the post office. It seems that Mary Wyatt (née Scrivener) was already working at the Forge, so she would have been familiar with the workings of the post office and there would have been no need to move it elsewhere. The Field Books of 1912-15 record John Wyatt leasing land from Edward Slater-Harrison, as follows: '2 closes of pasture & shed, traphouse & stable' between Hall Farm and The Forge.

By 1901, William Biggers at the Old Bake House had taken over the post office. The 1910 Valuation records: 'Fdk Plumb, tenant of Geo Kirby Whitton, 27 Norma Rd, Waterloo, Liverpool, Cott & Shop. Lease 2000 years from sometime in the reign of Queen Elizabeth. An old stone & thatched house with brick & gal.iron one story

The Old Forge, with Frederick Plumb (Matthew) in the cart. The smartly dressed boys were two of Kezia Whitton's grandsons, Arthur and Cuthbert, on a visit from Liverpool, 1890s. (Bill Plumb)

rear extension cont'g Gr fl. 2 sitting rms small cellar, sm. Pantry & back kitchen. 1st floor 4 brms. Adjoining the hse is an old stone & thatched smithy with brick fl. 2, forge & bellows rm in poor repair; adj is a stone & slated stable for 1 horse & carthouse- old & in moderate condition. Brick & gal. Iron pigstye, boiler, EC [earth closet]. Fair sized garden'. During Frederick Plumb's time at the Forge, a gang of metal-workers would sometimes come from London. They would stay with him, pay for the use of the forge and, with his help, make gates and other articles for local houses. They made the fine gates to Stratton Audley Hall and probably the ones leading to Manor Farm.

In 1923, Frederick purchased the property for £500 from George Whitton, with a mortgage of £222 15s @ 5 ½ % from the Grenville Lodge of the Oddfellows Friendly Society. He had seen a rent increase from £16 to £20 coming, and he paid the mortgage off in three years. After he died in 1930, Ernest Perrin rented the forge and continued the business until he bought Albert Jackman's smithy near the cricket ground in 1953. Frederick's son, William, continued to live at the Forge and he worked for Morris Motors at Cowley from 1926 to 1967. He was a brilliant mechanic and worked in the Experimental Division, where he was involved with Alec Issigonis, the creator of the Mini. After his death in 1973, his son, Bill, lived at the Forge until the 1990s. The Automobile Association sign on the front of the house was originally put up in about 1926, when it was common to put these signs on village

John and Kezia Whitton, with their sons, Alexander, left, and, right, George, Frederick Plumb is standing behind them, c.1888. (Bill Plumb)

forges. It was taken down in the Second World War but Bill Plumb found it in one of the sheds after the War and put it back up.[24]

MIDWAY was built by Bill Plumb in the early 1970s, in the orchard of The Forge, where his father, William, was still living.

ROSEMARY COTTAGE was built in 1952 on the site of an old thatched cottage. Jimmy Gerring, who was the sexton for many years, used to live here. Recently, the cottage has been demolished and replaced by two semi-detached cottages, called Rosemary and Primrose.

GANDERS is also on the site of an old thatched cottage.

ROSECROFT is the only eighteenth-century cottage to survive on the left side of Main Street. Cecil and Agnes Cross used to live here. Cecil was the butcher and his slaughter house was next door on the corner of what is now Crosslands. Agnes was the church organist for many years. There used to be a small cottage on the south side of Rosecroft.

FEDDANS, on the right, was built recently on the site of the old Gable Cottage, which was demolished. It was originally two eighteenth-century cottages, with its

Frederick Plumb with Thomas Deeley (in smock) in the garden of the Old Forge, note the privy in the background. c.1910. (Bill Plumb)

gable end fronting on to Main Street. This was common practice when there was limited frontage available on the main street and a cottage had to be squeezed into a very narrow space.

STONE GAP COTTAGE was the old tobacconists and confectioners shop run by Lizzie Grantham, from the 1930s until she retired in the late 1950s. Previously she lived in Bakery Cottage. It may be her in the photograph of Main Street in the 1920s. Bill Grantham recalls that she used to put her hand on the scales to make sure that she never gave the children too many sweets! Her sister lived with her and they are both remembered as large scary ladies by small boys buying sweets.

THE THATCHED COTTAGES, which include The Cottage and Fox Cottage (formerly Amberley), date from the late seventeenth century or early eighteenth century. The porches were added in the twentieth century. In recent times, the stonework has been refurbished and finely re-pointed in authentic fashion. The cottages have also been re-thatched recently, by a local thatcher, Neil Painting, who lives in the village- more like Victorian times when the village was largely self-supporting.

THE COTTAGE was originally two cottages. Gladys Hinks can just recall Sarah Butler Rennison, the letter-carrier, living in the left-hand one in the late 1920s. In her letter of 1919, Sarah seems to confirm this, 'You should just see them [weeds] in my garden in the street the same old garden that Dad [Richard Butler] used to have but I'm afraid I don't keep it so well as he had used to.'[25] She moved to Church Farm House (see below) for a while after that but returned to The Cottage in the late 1920s. It may be her standing outside the cottages in the 1920s photograph. In 1932 she moved to live with her son, William and his wife Beatrice, in Somerford Heynes, near Cirencester, where she died in 1933 (aged 82). There is an interesting comment by her daughter, Nellie Dean, in a letter written after her mother's death, 'I must tell you Somerford Heynes is like Fringford near Bicester, forgotten and forsaken.'![26]

FOX COTTAGE (formerly Amberley) was the home of James 'Jimmy' Grantham, who became a carrier in 1874, going to The George in Banbury every Thursday, and also to Bicester, Brackley, and Buckingham every week. On the left of the cottage is the old cart entrance with wide plank doors. Flora Thompson has a reference to him 'It was thought quite dashing to ride with Old Jimmy but frightfully extravagant, as the fare was sixpence. Most people preferred to go on foot and keep the sixpence to spend when they got there [Banbury].'[27] (See also Country Carriers in Chapter 7). Jimmy's father, also named James, was keeping the Butchers Arms in 1847, when he was also a baker. Jimmy's son, William, succeeded him as the local carrier but became a coal merchant in the 1920s until he retired in 1936. He lived on Main Street and kept his cart and, later, his coal lorry in a shed on the corner of Church Lane. The cottage was later the home of Gilbert Slatter, before he built Stonehaven (now Holly Cottage) further down Main Street

BAKERY COTTAGE was never a bakery; it was given its name because it had a bread oven, which was a common feature in old cottages.

FRINGFORD COTTAGE was built in 1938 by Miss Joyce Tomkinson. She was a great character and played a leading part in village life, as Chair of the Parish Council, Chair of Managers of the School, and President of the Cricket Club. During the Second World War she was Commandant of the Tusmore Hospital, a recovery home for wounded officers. She was greatly loved and a little feared by the village. She rode side-saddle to hounds into her early 70s and never missed a meet until a few months before her death.

FOLLY FIELDS was the site of Folly Barn, which belonged to the Sumners at Church Farm House until after the Second World War. The Buckingham family bought the barn and built the present house.

FOLLY COTTAGES date from the seventeenth or early eighteenth century, and were once a line of three thatched cottages. The porches were added in the twentieth century. Evacuees lived in No.1 during the Second World War. Mr and Mrs Dudley and their family lived in No.3. He was a butcher in Twyford, Buckinghamshire, and

Rosecroft, formerly home of Cecil Cross the butcher, with the butcher's shop on the right, 1950s. (Stephanie Maciejewski)

used to walk the five miles there and back each day to work. Nos.2 and 3 have romance attached to them, as they were made into one after Chris Singleton (No.3) married Jane (No.2) in the late 1970s. This caused some confusion for the milkman among others! More recently, the cottages have been sub-divided again.

BEAGLE COTTAGE dates from the seventeenth or early eighteenth century. There used to be three cottages here and you can see where some of the old doorways have been blocked up. Inside there are still three old winder staircases. The cottage has been renovated and re-thatched.

HOLLY COTTAGE, opposite, formerly Stonehaven, was built on the site of a thatched cottage by Gilbert Slatter, who formerly lived in Amberley Cottage. Bill and Hannah Grantham lived here in the 1940s for a rent of 3s.(15p) per week and had no electricity until 1948.

ST MICHAEL'S CLOSE was developed in the early 1970s, after the demolition of Mansfield Yard.

Church End
DAIRY COTTAGE was built quite recently on a plot which had been marked out for a house after the demolition of Mansfield Yard. The Sumners had a dairy here until 1965, and supplied the village with milk.

MANSFIELD YARD: in the early 1970s this group of old cottages was all demolished, except for Yew Tree Cottage, which has since been enlarged. The Yard included the former Mansfield's grocery store (see Village Shops in Chapter 7). The store was run by John and Mary Mansfield and, as noted above, it was their son, Frederick, who went to Courteenhall Grammar School with the Whitton boys. He was initially a carpenter and went on to become a railway coach finisher at Wolverton, Northants. There is no evidence that any of the other Mansfield children went to Courteenhall. After John's death in 1886, Mary continued to run the grocery store, 'Mansfield, Grocer and Licensed Dealers in Tobacco', until she died in 1914, so Flora would have known her and the store well.

The Yard was commonly known as "Birdie Cage" after Margaret Bird, one of the residents. William Elderfield, who had a thriving clock and watch repair business, lived in one of the cottages and had a separate workshop in the Yard. He used to do repairs for Harrods in London in addition to all his local work. Older residents recall the hundreds of pounds' worth of clocks and watches ticking away in his workshop. William was a blacksmith when he joined the army during the First World War. His delicate touch was discovered then and he was trained as a watchmaker/repairer.

Three new cottages were built on the site of the old Yard. The three cottages opposite were built in the 1960s.

YEW TREE COTTAGE, in Mansfield Yard, was built by David Mansfield in the late nineteenth century and his name is still carved above the fireplace. Ernest and Emily Hinks used to live here with their daughter, Gladys, as did her grandparents before them. Emily, and later Gladys, ran a small shop. Gladys was the cook at the Old School and later at the Bicester Army Base, and she still lives in St Michael's Close, aged 96. She recalls that her father, who was a carpenter by trade, also kept pigs and hens in a paddock leased from John Dewar-Harrison next to the Yard. After the First World War, when it was very difficult to find employment, Ernest used to 'get on his bike' and cycle to Coventry to look for work. During the Second World War he was a ganger employed by the RAF to do all sorts of 'rural jobs' on the Shelswell airfield.

The VILLAGE PUMP, opposite Mansfield Yard, was for use by this end of the village until the arrival of mains water c.1960. It was thought that the pump water was infected by the trees, so people continued to use water from the wells for drinking. There were a great number of wells in the village, including no less than three at the Forge. The thatched cover was put over the pump in memory of Douglas Crowther, who died in 1987. It has been re-thatched recently.

THE LODGE was built in the Gothic style for Henry Chinnery in 1898, by the firm of Thomas Grimsley of Bicester, when he was rebuilding Fringford Manor. Jim Wyatt lived here with his family when he took over the tenancy of Manor Farm in 1940,

Mansfield Yard, with Yew Tree Cottage on the right, Church End. The Yard, except for Yew Tree Cottage, was demolished in the early 1970s. (Gladys Hinks)

Granny Elizabeth Hinks with her lace bobbins, like Queenie in Lark Rise. She is sitting with William 'Joe' Spacey in front of her cottage in Mansfield Yard, late 1920s. (Gladys Hinks)

and his grandson, Mark, lives here now. On the corner, there used to be two sets of gates to the Manor, which were erected by the Chinnerys in 1898-99.

FRINGFORD MANOR (formerly Manor Farm) was simply an old farmhouse, until a major conversion in 1898-99 by Henry Chinnery, who leased the Manor and its lands from Edward Slater-Harrison. By 1851 Thomas Simons was farming here. By 1861 his son, John, had succeeded him, and he continued to farm here until his death in 1896 (see Chapter 4). Shortly after this, there are some interesting comments in the surviving letters of Kezia Whitton.[28] On 26 March 1897 she attended 'Mr Simons sale' and found the old place 'in a terrible dilapidated state now everything is took off the walls.' By 14 November 1897, 'a Mr Chinnery has took Mr Simons house....or rather the Manor house as it is called now.'

By 6 February 1898, 'there are about 50 people, Workmen of all classes down at the manor house.' She mentions new stables and 'they are making a new coach road round to the front, by the churchyard wall, and are thinking of putting a lodge again [sic] the Swing gate, and at least 2 more cottages.' The Chinnerys did build the Lodge and put up new gates. They also built a number of cottages. 'They have already built a new bridge down again [sic] Fridays Meadow (where the little narrow one was) to drive out from it by the Morrell [Newton Morrell] to this new station at Barley Fields [Finmere Station, which opened in March 1899] - but whether it will be a public road or not is a matter of (word deleted).' It did not become a public road, and, after the Second World War, further proposals were also unsuccessful. The Council wished to build a through road to Newton Morrell, so that Fringford would not be a cul-de-sac. Miss Joyce Tomkinson played a major role in thwarting these proposals for what she called 'a Silverstone racetrack' by buying two fields behind her house, Fringford Cottage, which were along the proposed route. After Henry's death in 1914, his widow, Marion, lived in the Manor until her death in 1938. Her son, Ellis, continued to farm here after the 1914-18 War, until he moved to Fringford House on Rectory Lane in 1921.

During the Second World War, a convent school was evacuated from Norwood, the juniors to Fringford Manor and the seniors to Swift's House, Stoke Lyne. Every Sunday both schools used to walk in crocodile to the Holy Trinity Catholic Chapel in Hethe, the juniors in dark brown uniforms, the seniors in dark blue ones. In 1948 John Dewar-Harrison wanted to build new houses for some of his workers. When he found that this was impossible because of material shortages after the War, he converted the Manor into six houses for them. In No.6 Mrs Laura Powell ran the Post Office (said to be the smallest in England) from 1953 to 1986. In the 1980s, further conversions were made to the west barns, the Manor's former milking parlour, and in the stable yard, to provide more housing.

MANOR FARM was built in the 1980s by Jim Wyatt, on the site of the Manor's kitchen garden and orchard. After Ellis Chinnery moved to Fringford House in 1921,

Mansfield's grocery store, Church End, early 1900s. (Peter Morrall)

Walter Woodrow, who lived in The Lodge, acted as his bailiff, while Cecil Cross farmed the Manor's land until 1940 when Jim Wyatt took over. In 1967 he inherited the farmlands from John Dewar-Harrison. After Jim Wyatt's death in 1971, his son, John, continued to farm here. In 1973 he built Manor Farm on the site of the old Manor's orchard and kitchen gardens. In the 1980s, he saw to the development of Manor Road. In 1991 he sold the farm and moved to Dadford, near Stowe, where he farms with his sons. Jane Petry now runs a herb farm here.

Walk down to the end of the road and look into the private courtyard.

The coachman and other staff of the Chinnerys lived here. The grooms' mess room and the tack room (Coach House Cottage) were on the right next to the old Coach House. Straight ahead is Gardener's Cottage, and the Old Stables are on the left.

Walk back to the churchyard.

The CHURCHYARD was enlarged in 1875 and 1906 by gifts of land from Eton College and the Harrison family. John Whitton made the entrance gate c.1870 and you can still see the Whitton name on it. Just inside the gate on the right, you can see a cast-iron cross marking the grave of Zilpha Hinks (the servant Zillah in *Lark Rise*). These unusual cast-iron crosses, which you can see over a number of the graves, date from between 1888 and 1937. There are more crosses of this type in Fringford (24) than anywhere else in Oxfordshire.[29] They were available nationally

A photograph taken from Fringford church tower, showing the Lodge and Mansfield's store on the right, early 1900s. (Peter Morrall)

in various forms and they were very popular because they were much cheaper than stone memorials. Five of the Fringford crosses were made at Stratford-on-Avon by the John Smith Company. On the left, the War Memorial, that stands on the base of the old medieval cross, records the names of the seven men who gave their lives in the two World Wars. The memorial was erected in time for the Service of Remembrance on 11 November 1923. There are plans to refurbish it and re-engrave the names shortly. To the north of the church, you can see three substantial gravestones of the Whitton family: Kezia and John, and their son, Alexander, who died on the Gold Coast, aged 24.

ST MICHAEL and ALL ANGELS CHURCH may stand on the site of an early wooden building. However, the earliest evidence yet found dates from the early twelfth century (1103), when Baron Manasses Arsic, lord of Fringford, built a new church and granted it to the Priory of Black Monks, which he had founded at Cogges, near Witney.

12th to 13th century: the two northern arches of the nave and the plain doorway into the vestry date from this period. The three southern arches probably date from the thirteenth century. Two of the south pillars are decorated with grotesque heads, men's heads on one of them making faces at some women's heads on the opposite pillar. These are probably a later thirteenth-century carver's joke! The twelfth-century south doorway and porch were replaced with a copy in the nineteenth century.

St Michael and All Angels Church, 1930s. (OCC)

15th century: the roughly carved rood-screen dates from this period. Originally there must have been a low gate to the chancel, as you can see the marks where the hinges would have fitted. It must have been removed when the chancel was rebuilt in the nineteenth century and its floor level raised. The earlier existence of a gate is not surprising as the chancel was seen as the preserve of the priest, while the nave was for the laity.

18th century: on the wall of the north aisle, there are memorials to two members of the Addington family of Hall Farm. As we have seen above, a descendent, Dr Anthony Addington (1718-90), was doctor to William Pitt 'The Elder' (the first Earl of Chatham) and to George III. Fringford has been a Crown living since 1775.

19th century: the church was largely rebuilt in this period, mainly thanks to three of its rectors. From 1814 to 1894, Fringford was fortunate to enjoy the considerable personal wealth, intellectual ability and social standing of three 'regal rectors':
    Henry Roundell (1814-52), Henry Fane de Salis (1852-73) and Cadwallader Coker (1873-94). In the chancel, there are memorials on the north wall to Henry and Elizabeth Roundell and to Cadwallader and Emily Coker. On the south wall, there is one to the Revd John Russell Greenhill (1756-1813) and his wife Elizabeth. A new chancel was built in 1821, the north aisle in 1829, and in 1831 the present stone tower was constructed by Daniel Mansfield of Hethe to replace the wooden belfry. In 1842, the pulpit was installed, using sixteenth-century carved panels from neighbouring Hardwick manor, and the vestry was built. In 1856, under the guidance of the

Gravestones erected in Fringford churchyard to the memory of John and Kezia Whitton, and their son, Alexander Whitton, who died of fever in 1889 and is buried at Accra on the African Gold Coast.

Diocesan architect, G.E.Street, the south aisle was enlarged and the south doorway and porch restored. In 1876, the clock was installed by William Beesley of Finmere.

Fonts: there are two fonts in the south aisle. The older one, possibly fifteenth-century, was originally three-sided and only later cut into an octagon shape. It was presented by the Revd Henry Roundell, who had been given it by his brother-in-law, the Revd William Palmer of Mixbury. However, in 1890 it was standing in the churchyard, having been superseded in 1880 by a new one, a memorial to Mrs Anne King, of Waterloo Farm. This one now stands by the pulpit, and the old font has pride of place by the south door.

Twentieth century: in 1905, Henry Chinnery paid for the north chapel to be rebuilt. Two clerestory windows were added, the ceiling was re-decorated, and stained glass was placed in the east window. The angel fresco behind the altar was painted in 1902. Restoration in 2004 revealed that the artist's name was T.F.M.Sheard, who lived in the Vale of White Horse and exhibited fourteen works at the Royal Academy between 1891 and 1903. The fine altar here was given by Mrs Marjorie Chinnery in 1972, and some local people still refer to the north aisle as the 'Chinnery Chapel'.

Fringford Manor, showing the fine front terrace, 1922. (Bill Plumb)

The carvings: in 1839, John Rogers, the organist and village carpenter, carved new seats for the nave. He also made the fine casing for the new organ, which had been given by the Revd Henry de Salis in 1853. The beautiful carving on the pew-ends was done before the First World War by Charlie Freeman, who also carved the whole vestry wall and the choir stalls. He seems to have emigrated in the 1890s to Canada, where his feet were ruined by frostbite. He had returned to Fringford by 1901, to an old cottage next to the Old School where his parents had kept a sweet shop and pastured sheep on the Green. He became wood carver to the Church and to his patron, Henry Chinnery, and caretaker of the Reading Room, now the Village Hall, which Mr Chinnery had built for the village in 1901. He used to hobble down to the Church each day with the aid of two sticks and two iron callipers on his legs, and did most of his work lying down in the aisles. He died in 1912.

The stained glass: there was so much stained glass installed in the nineteenth century that, as a later rector said, 'no one can now read his prayer book without electric light'! The Roundell family filled all the windows in the chancel. In the north aisle, one window was dedicated in 1898 to Cadwallader Coker and his family and another one to John Dewar, who was killed in the Boer War in 1900.

The bells: one of the bells was cast by R.Atton of Buckingham in 1617 and two of them by R.Chandler in 1702. The small Sanctus bell was cast c.1800 by Robert Wills of Aldbourne in Wiltshire. The peal was re-hung in 1831 when the wooden belfry was removed and the existing stone tower was built by Daniel Mansfield. Unfortunately, because of the present dilapidated state of the tower, the bells can no longer be rung properly.

Owen Judd, in front of Church Farm House, 1920. (Vera Raby)

The Flora Thompson Plaque: On 4th July 2010, a plaque to commemorate Flora Thompson's years in Fringford from 1891 to 1897 was unveiled by Linda Bassett (who played Queenie in the television adaptation of *Lark Rise*), on the wall by the south door. The plaque of Welsh blue slate was sculpted by Giles Macdonald of Banbury. Flora was buried in Dartmouth in 1947, alongside her son, Peter, who had been killed when his ship was torpedoed in 1941.

The church is now one of ten in the Shelswell Benefice in the Diocese of Oxford, that are combined under one rector. There are plans for substantial improvements to the church, including access to a water supply, a toilet, a servery, and glass panels between the nave and the north chapel. See Chapter 5 for more about the Church and Clergy.

Leave the churchyard by the small gate at the north-west corner and enter Church Lane.
As you leave, note the memorial on the right to the Revd Coker and members of his family, including his grandson, Lewis, who died in 1879, aged 19, at Ekowe in South Africa. He was serving as a midshipman in the Naval Brigade on HMS *Active* during the Anglo-Zulu Wars. The Cokers were a wealthy family from Bicester and many of them are commemorated in St Edburg's Church there.

Church Lane
As a result of the changes in occupancy over the last 150 years, the lane has been variously called Judds Lane, Sumners Lane and now Church Lane.

Sarah Butler Rennison, in the back garden of Church Farm House, early 1920s.
(Elizabeth Bagley)

CHURCH FARM HOUSE, formerly Eton College Farm, is believed to be a timber-framed farmhouse of the sixteenth or seventeenth century but there may well have been earlier farm buildings. The site used to be owned by Eton College, possibly as early as 1441 when they acquired the manor in Cottisford. In the 1890s, the College's property in Fringford still comprised 'a mill and closes adjoining, together with four fields and a farmhouse (now converted into cottages) near the Church.'[30]

The newel staircase on the back of the house is likely to be pre-1750. The Judd family had a long connection with the village from at least the early nineteenth century and they lived here as tenants from c.1860 to 1921.They were mostly agricultural labourers and coal hauliers. Thomas Judd was the parish clerk for thirty-seven years from the late 1860s for an annual fee of £5, also supplying coal, gravel,

Aerial view of the Old Rectory and Prentice's Yard gardens, 1976. (Charles Hebditch)

wood and straw, sweeping the flues and ringing the bells. He used to collect coal from Finmere station and store it in bunkers in the farmyard.

The Fringford Valuation Forms 37 (1913) record Reuben Judd as the occupier and sub-tenant of J.S.Mansfield, with some 8 acres, and Eton College still the owner. The Field Books (1913-15) record 'Hse & bldgs with 2 small pasture fields. Hse containing 4 bedrms 2 attics 3 living rms. Pantry with stabling, cattle shed, Chaff house & hovel. One hovel used for cycle repairing shop. Old property in fair repair.
Map shows an open cart shed in present rockery area.' In 1921, the College sold the farm to Harold Judd, when they were selling all their remaining property in Fringford and Cottisford. Sarah Butler Rennison, the letter-carrier, was living in the south end cottage by the early 1920s, after moving from The Cottage on Main Street. This is when her photograph was taken in the back garden, and it shows a very strong and determined lady. It may have been taken by Harold Judd, as he was apparently trying his hand at photography; another photograph by 'H.Judd, Photographer' has surfaced recently.[31] We shall see more of Sarah in Chapter 7.

From 1928 to 1965 the Sumners farmed here and ran a dairy but the house was still divided into three cottages. By 1965, the property was in a very poor state of repair. Fortunately, in the late 1960s, the new owner restored and extended the front of the house, and made it into one dwelling again. The remains of the old granary were pulled down in the early 1980s, when Paddy McMahon, the Irish show jumper, built an annexe for his grooms on the south end. The remains of the bunkers and some lumps of coal were found in 1990, after McMahon sold the property and moved the wooden stables to his new property, Forge Mill House. The annexe has now been incorporated into the main house, the old stables have been largely rebuilt and the old cowshed restored.

ROSEMARY COTTAGE, opposite, is a late Victorian cottage built by the rector, the Revd Coker. 'Snobby' Judd, a shoemaker and an older brother of Reuben at Church Farm House, lived here until his death in 1935.

FORGE MILL HOUSE was built in 1990-91 by Paddy McMahon after he sold Church Farm House. It was named after his famous horse, Penward Forge Mill.

CHURCH COTTAGES, Nos.1 and 2, are late Victorian cottages, built by the Revd Coker. No.2 was extended in the 1990s.

Take the small footpath on the right after Church Cottages.
GHOST ALLEY is an apt name for what was once a rather spooky path. Perhaps there is also a ghost from the Civil War skirmish near Fringford in March 1645 when the Royalists were retreating from Finmere? Another possible explanation is that this was the route of the hand-bier for 'walking funerals' from the undertaker, Billy Judd in Rectory Lane. Notice the long garden on the left. It was here that all the cottages in Prentice's Yard had their gardens and hovels [toilets] over on the far side. On the right is the long boundary wall of the Old Rectory garden.

Rectory Lane
RECTORY LANE is a very old road, probably used by Saxon drovers in the eighth century. They used to bring their sheep from Wales and the West to Brackley, which was a thriving wool centre. The old lane went round to the left of Bancroft and down across the field to 'Fera's Ford' and up to Willaston. There were still traces of a stone-paved way to Willaston in the nineteenth century. In the summer of 1891, the young Flora Timms would have taken this route from the post office to Shelswell Manor, to be admitted to her position by Edward Slater-Harrison (Sir Timothy in *Lark Rise*).

THE OLD RECTORY was a mere thatched cottage in 1756, too small for the new rector's family. 'As late as 1818 the rectory house consisted only of two small rooms, with kitchen and scullery, on the ground floor, with bedrooms above. Mr Roundell [Revd Henry Roundell, 1814-52] in that year added the larger rooms on the east side, and refaced the old house with local stone. In 1873 the present rector, Mr Coker [Revd Cadwallader Coker, 1878-94] built out a small study on the opposite side, and converted one of the small rooms of the old house into an entrance-hall.'[32] The additions by Mr Roundell cost £2,098, and he made further additions later. The old stables and coach-house used to be on the west side.

   The drive to the Rectory used to go round to the left of Bancroft, which was an orchard, and up to the old front of the house. Traces of the old front door and doorstep can still be seen, where there is a curve in the stonework. A cart-track used to cross Bancroft field and connect the Rectory to the Hethe road. This was still being driven by the rector in living memory. In 1913, the Field Books record the Revd R.D.L.Clarke occupying the house and gardens with some 2 acres. He also owned glebe land, including Glebe Farm (see Chapter 4) and land around Fringford Bridge, including the old allotments. The rectory has been sold recently and a substantial refurbishment has just been completed (2015).

BANCROFT: in the 1960s, the Bancroft orchard was sold to Len Standen, who built a house here in 1964, on his retirement as head-teacher of the Old School. In 1853, the Revd de Salis noted 'No school room. Half of the Old Tithe Barn fitted up by me as a School House for which purpose it now answers very well'. There were 20 children here and 20 at an infant school, until the National School was built in 1866. There is an old bell on the roof of the rectory, which may have been used to call these children to their lessons. The present owners have enlarged the house substantially and modernised the old barn.

FRINGFORD HOUSE, formerly Rectory Cottage or The Cottage, used to be on glebe land owned by the rector. The small central core dates from the seventeenth century, while the south wing was added in the late nineteenth century. The house was rented to various tenants, until Ellis and Katharine Chinnery bought it in 1921 when they moved from the Manor. They changed the name and built significant extensions on the north end, west side, and a further one on the south side.
CANDLEFORD MEWS, including the Pump House and the Coach House, used to be the stables and outbuildings for Fringford House. When Katharine Chinnery died in 1978, they were converted and Candleford Cottage was built at the end of the Mews.

MEADOW VIEW, opposite the Rectory gates, was part of a row of five cottages built in the eighteenth century or earlier. The brick second storey seems to have been added later. This was the home of Billy Judd, the undertaker, who was also chauffeur to the Chinnerys and a carpenter/handyman. Billy was a great village character, who is remembered as a 'loveable rogue' and a great drinker, who could be too clever for his own good! There was nothing mechanical or electrical that he could not fix. He had the first wireless in the village and used to charge up batteries for others. He drove his own Bullnose Morris, one of the first cars in the village. He could be extremely smart, whether dressed as the undertaker or chauffeuring the Chinnerys.

PRENTICE'S YARD was named after William Prentice, a butcher from Bicester, who bought it from Thomas Gibbard of Laurels Farm in April 1902 for £310. The group of nine cottages had also been sold as a block in 1875,, when it was known as Franklin's Yard. The Yard used to have another row of three or four cottages on the edge of the lane. The first one was a grocery shop, remembered as 'Mrs Carey's', where there used to be a chocolate machine on a post outside the shop. The shop remained open until the row of cottages was demolished and Prentice's Yard was split up in the early 1950s.

STABLE COTTAGE (formerly Samarkand): 'Granny Wright' had a small sweetshop in part of the cottage. The House family formerly occupied the rear of the cottage. Ebenezer Sirett and Edie Price lived next door.

MAVIS HOUSE was formerly two cottages, which were occupied by the Cherry and Timms families. It has now been modernised and extended on the right-hand end.

LITTLE PADDOCK is a mid-1990s development.

PUMP COTTAGE is named after the pump, which was used by the residents on Rectory Lane and by the Old School. In 1944, the head teacher, Harold Corfe, commented for the benefit of his successor: 'the pump in the scullery and the water from it not fit to poison pigs. All the drinking water in buckets from village pump – 50 yards.'[33]

VIXEN COTTAGE: note the blocked door and window still visible on the north wall and some alterations to the south wall. There used to be two other small stone cottages on the south side, one of which was occupied by Miss Hitchcock, who ran a small shop. Henry Taylor, of Waterloo Farm, demolished both the cottages after he bought them in the 1970s, apparently because he needed the stone to build some walls.

BOND'S COTTAGES next door, at right angles to the Lane, are much altered. Henry Taylor bought the two brick cottages for £100 each when he bought Vixen Cottage. Albert Jackman, the farrier, used to occupy one of them.

FARRIERS CLOSE, which originally would have been part of the Green, was developed at the end of the 1990s. Excavations prior to the development revealed a series of Iron Age and Romano-British boundary ditches. These were overlain by a further series of ditches of the tenth or eleventh century, including a possible domestic enclosure. This phase was superseded in the twelfth century by ridge-and-furrow ploughing. This continued until the second half of the thirteenth century when three stone buildings were constructed. One of these appears to have been a farrier's workshop, hence the new name of the Close. It is possible that the buildings formed part of a manorial complex. In the middle of the fourteenth century the buildings seem to have been abandoned and the whole area converted to pasture. This was the period of the Black Death and other plagues, which resulted in large-scale depopulation.

PRINGLE COTTAGE was probably built in the eighteenth century. The south end and the bay window were added in the 1950s, when an old barn was removed. At the same time,, the north end, which used to be a workshop, was converted. Members of the Price family lived here and next door in Rose Cottage from the 1860s. They rented the copse across the road by the Old School House as a garden. Ernest, like many of the Price family, was a painter, plumber and decorator. Ernest and Ellen Price also ran the Post Office here from 1910, after it moved from the Old Bake House. After Ernest's death in 1945, Ellen continued to run it until 1953, with help from her daughter-in-law, Elsie. There used to be a post-box, and later a telephone kiosk by the front gate. By a stroke of good fortune, some of the old Price ledgers survived in the attic. They provide a fascinating record of their customers and work from 1869 until the early 1900s (see Chapter 8).

ROSE COTTAGE was originally a thatched cottage, probably built in the eighteenth century. During the Second World War, Sam Goddard, a schoolmaster who came with the evacuees, lived in one half, while Lily Price was living in the other half. She was the infants' teacher and was described by the headmaster, Mr Corfe, as follows: 'no "qualifications" but jolly good - leave her to it - a bit temperamental but a solid worker who does jolly well.'

You can now retrace your steps to the Green and back to the Butchers Arms.

Chapter 3 footnotes

[17] *Lark Rise*, 524.
[18] Blomfield, *Fringford*, 26.
[19] *Bicester Advertiser*, 4 June 1901.
[20] Blomfield, *Fringford*, 16.
[21] Blomfield, *Fringford*, 20.
[22] *Lark Rise*, 395-5.
[23] Letter from Kezia Whitton to her son, George, 6 February 1898.
[24] I am indebted to Bill Plumb for much of the information in these paragraphs.
[25] Letter from Sarah Butler Rennison to her brother, Thomas Butler, c.1916.
[26] Letter from Nellie Dean to Thomas Butler and Family, 9 February 1933.
[27] *Lark Rise*, 254.
[28] Letters from Kezia Whitton to her son, George, 26 March 1897, 14 November 1897 and 6 February 1898.
[29] Letter from Tony and Mary Yoward to Mrs E.M.B.Young, 23 September 1987.
[30] Blomfield, *Fringford*, 21.
[31] I am indebted to David Judd for this information.
[32] Blomfield, *Fringford*, 44.
[33] Lertter from H.A.Corfe to J.L.Standen, 11 June 1944.

Chapter 4

The Farms

In 1851, there were ten active farms in Fringford: Eton College (later Church Farm), Green, Hall, Laurels, and Manor farms in the village, and outlying farms at Cotmore (later Moat Farm), Cotmore House, Fringford Lodge, Glebe, Moat and Waterloo. In 1939 there were still nine active farms: Church, Hall, Laurels, and Manor farms in the village, and the outlying Cotmore, Fringford Lodge, Glebe, Moat and Waterloo farms. The big difference between the two dates is that, with the growth of mechanisation, the farms were no longer so labour intensive by 1939. Today, there are only four farms, Hall Farm, The Laurels, Moat Farm and Waterloo Farm. The numbers for the individual farms below show how labour intensive they were in the 1850s and 1860s.

The Village Farms

(a) Church Farm (formerly Eton College Farm)

As has been noted, this site used to be owned by Eton College, possibly as early as 1441. The present timber-framed farmhouse dates from the sixteenth or seventeenth century but there may well have been earlier farm buildings. In the 1890s, Eton College's property in Fringford still comprised 'a mill and closes adjoining, together with four fields and a farmhouse (now converted into cottages) near the Church.'[34] From about 1860 to 1921 the Judd family, who were mostly agricultural labourers and coal hauliers, lived here as tenants. In the 1890s they had some 8 acres but the Field Books (1912-15) record just 2 small pasture fields. In 1921, the College sold the farm to Harold Judd, when they were selling all their remaining property in Fringford and Cottisford. He sold the property in the same year, and there was then a variety of occupants until the Sumners bought it in 1928. They farmed here and ran a dairy, supplying the village with milk, until 1965. None of the subsequent owners have been farmers.

(b) Green Farm

The farmhouse is listed as late seventeenth century, with eighteenth-century additions. Parts, including an old floor, may be earlier. The Domesday Valuation and Field Books (Appendix 2) record Ann & Thomas Gibbard as tenants of Edward Slater-Harrison, with 'Farm house, bldgs, & land known as Flower Farm' with some 62 acres. Thomas died in 1938 and by the late 1930s the building had been

subdivided and Walter Wilkins and Hubert Hancock were living here as tenants. As
has been noted, Wilkins farmed the land, while 'Bert' Hancock took over the bakery
at the Old Bake House. In 1959/60 the Wilkins moved out and Roy Tew moved from
his farm in Godington into the main house. His son, Norman, continued to farm in
Godington but he also farmed some land in Fringford. Roy continued to live in the
farm house with his housekeeper until the early 1980s. He then moved into Green
Farm Cottage next door, where he stayed until his death in the early 1990s.

(c) Hall Farm (formerly Fringford Hall Farm)

As previously mentioned, the Addington family have owned the farm for some 400
years. For much of the nineteenth century and the first half of the twentieth century
the Mansfield family farmed here. In 1861 John Mansfield was farming 200 acres
with 9 men and 4 boys. In 1871 Edwin Mansfield was farming 130 acres with 6 men,
2 boys and 1 girl. By 1883 the farm was in the name of Wm Mansfield (Exors), and
occupied by a bailiff and servants. The 1910 Domesday Valuation records George
Mansfield, as tenant of Viscount Sidmouth, with 122 acres, and 'A Farm House &
Bldgs, arable & pasture lands very excellent over the Parish in small quantities thro'
Fr Parish.' It also states that the house is 'severed from the bulk of the land'. Lovell
Buckingham took the farm over from Thomas Mansfield in the late 1930s and farmed
it with his sons until Ian Thomas took over the tenancy in March 1965. His son,
Charlie, now runs the farm, with some 100 acres, together with 'Fringford Feeds,
Horse, Pet and Poultry Supplies'.

(d) Laurels Farm (now Laurels Farmhouse)

The farmhouse is listed as late seventeenth or early eighteenth century, although
some parts may be earlier. As has been noted, George Gibbard farmed here from the
1850s and in 1861 he was farming '50 acres with 3 men and 1 boy'. In the 1883 Kelly's
Directory he was described as brewer, farmer and maltster. After his death in 1894,
his widow, Ann, farmed it with her son, Thomas. The Domesday Valuation and Field
Books record them as tenants of Henry Chinnery, farming some 49 acres. The
Gibbards continued to farm here until Thomas died in 1938, when Albert Wise
bought the farm. In the 1980s, some of the farmland was sold to allow the new
houses, behind the farmhouse, to be built. In the 1990s, Richard Wise sold Laurels
Farm and built a new farmhouse, The Laurels, on the back road leading to
Caversfield.

(e) Fringford Manor (formerly Manor Farm)

In 1851, Thomas Simons was farming here on 276 acres with 7 labourers. By 1861,
his son, John, was farming 275 acres with 7 men and 3 boys, but by 1871 he was only
farming 170 acres, with 7 men and 2 boys. He continued to farm here until his death
in 1896. As has been noted, by 14 November 1897, 'a Mr Chinnery has took Mr
Simons house or rather the Manor house as it is called now.'[35] The Valuation Book

of 1910 records HJ [Henry] Chinnery holding the 'hse & bldgs', with some 5 acres, and his son, EH [Ellis], holding 117 acres of land, and the 1911 census records Ellis as a farmer. However, the Valuation Form 37, which was completed in 1915, still records Henry Chinnery holding some 138 acres with 'House Wage Cottage buildings & land.'

This must be a mistake, as Henry died in 1914, while Ellis continued to live and farm at the Manor until 1921, when he moved to Fringford House on Rectory Lane. Walter Woodrow then acted as his bailiff, while Cecil Cross, the butcher, farmed the Manor's land until 1940, when Jim Wyatt took over. As has been noted, in 1967 he inherited the farmlands from John Dewar-Harrison. After Jim's death in 1971, his son, John, continued to farm here and in 1973 he built Manor Farm on the site of the Manor's orchard and kitchen gardens. In 1991, he sold the property to Jane Petry, who now runs a herb farm here. He moved to Dadford, near Stowe, where he farms with his sons.

The Outlying Farms

(a) Cotmore

Cotmore, alias Cotemore, was the manor of the De Greys in the thirteenth century but was no more than a few scattered cottages until the early nineteenth century. In 1868, William W.M. Dewar, who had married Augusta Slater-Harrison, bought part of the estate from his father-in-law, John Slater-Harrison, and built the present Cotmore House. In 1871, he was farming 268 acres with 9 men and 3 boys. After William's death in 1903, Augusta continued to live at Cotmore House until her death in 1911. The Valuation Book of 1910 shows her farming 96 acres. One of her sons, Charles Gilbert, succeeded her and farmed there until his death in 1935. Robert Edward Field-Marsham, M.F.H. then lived there until the Second World War.

In 1941, Hugh and Gladys Meyrick-Jones moved to Cotmore from The Willows farm in Stratton Audley, along with their five daughters, Sheila, Daphne, Audrey, Aileen and Maureen. Hugh died in 1942 but the girls continued to run the 100 acre farm. The house was converted into flats in the early 1950s. After the girls married, Gladys continued to live in one of the flats, while Dick and Aileen Rymer, from Myddle Farm in Mixbury, ran the farm. In 1967, Cotmore was bought by the estate of John Towler who had been married to Maureen Meyrick-Jones. Recently Philippa Taylor, of Waterloo Farm, has bought Cotmore House from the estate.

(b) Fringford Lodge

Fringford Lodge, formerly Fringford House, is on the site of an old Roman villa, and title-deeds date from 1597. It was a part of Cotmore, which for a long time formed a separate estate of some 62 acres, on the edge of the parish adjoining the boundary stream. The chief part of the house, with barns, stables and other outbuildings, was erected in the early 1800s. In 1851, Fringford House Farm, with some 64 acres, was

Grace Dewar with her children in pony trap, Cotmore House, 1904/5. (Diana Joslin)

being farmed by Henry Parrot, and one labourer, together with Mary Smith, employed in agriculture with a son, aged 16, a labourer. In 1873, the Revd Edward Withington bought the estate. In 1891 he was living in Fringford House, while Sam Baughan (aged 58), bailiff, was in Fringford House Farm, and William Harwood (aged 30), coachman, in Fringford House Cottage. By 1891, Edward Withington had 'added to the house its eastern wing, and greatly improved its general appearance, and given it the new name it now bears "Fringford Lodge".'[36] In 1901, Samuel Baughan (68) was still the farm bailiff, while his son, Walter (27), coachman, was living in the cottage. There were also 3 labourers living in the cottages. The Valuation Book of 1910 records Baughan farming some 59 acres.

Frederick Withington (1869-1951) succeeded his father in 1901 but did not live at the Lodge until later. He achieved fame in the equestrian world for his remarkable link with the Grand National. After his education at Eton, he became a leading amateur jockey. On giving up riding in 1899, he trained steeplechase horses at Danebury, near Stockbridge, Hampshire. In about 1920 he moved back to Oxfordshire, first to Lodge Farm, Fritwell and then to the family home at Fringford Lodge. His major success came in 1908, when he had the first two home in the Grand National, the only time that this has been achieved.

The story of Rubio's victory in the 1908 Grand National is a romantic one. He won three races in 1903 but broke down badly. An extraordinary decision was then taken to send him to the landlord of the Prospect Arms in Towcester, where he would pull an omnibus in a harness in order to ferry guests between the station and the hotel. This was so successful that he was back in training in 1906. In 1908, he was entered for the Grand National but as the second string in the stable to the favourite, Mattie Macgregor. In the event he won by ten lengths from Mattie Macgregor, the only time that the first two horses have come from the same stable. In the 1920s, Vivian Hugh-Smith, subsequently created Baron Bicester of Tusmore in 1938, and Colonel E.H.Wyndham of Caversfield House, Bicester, both became patrons of Fred Withington. The Colonel owned a horse called Red Splash, which Fred trained to win the first running of the Cheltenham Gold Cup in 1924. The Fred Withington Chase was run at Cheltenham in his memory for many years.

The Field Books (1913-15) record Frederick's stud groom, F.Holford, with 'hse & stabling, gdn grds & grooms cott & gdn.' In the 1920s, Mrs Smyly, of the Rigden brewing family, who lived at Stratton Audley Hall, bought the Lodge from him, as a hunting box. Later her daughter, Betty Rigden, who was a well-known breeder of horses, lived and farmed there. She was part-owner of Windmill Girl, who was mother of two Derby winners, Blakeney (1969) and Morston (1973). Both were trained by Arthur Budgett of Kirtlington. After Betty Rigden's death, her daughter, Susan Haines, inherited the property but there have been no further farming or racing connections here.

(c) Glebe Farm (formerly Rectory Farm)

'By the Enclosure Act of 1761.. it was also provided that a homestead with a barn, stables and other outbuildings should be erected on the land allotted as glebe, at a cost of £200, which sum was to be advanced by Mr Fulke Greville on condition of his receiving from the glebe as much land as should be considered of equal value. Thus the Rectory Farm had its commencement.'[37]

In 1851, Henry Tubb was farming 160 acres here, with 7 labourers. By 1861, he was farming 200 acres with 8 men and 2 boys. In 1891, the farm was occupied by Henry Busby, farm servant, and the farm cottages by John Heritage, shepherd. In 1901, John Keen was the farmer. The Field Books (1913-15) record his son, John G. Keen, with 'Glebe Fmhse, 2 cottages, bldgs & land' farming some 174 acres. After he retired from farming in 1917, Alfred Taylor took over the farm, initially as a tenant. He had been a blacksmith in Murcott on Otmoor originally but he was keen to start farming. He was also a shrewd buyer of property, and during the Second World War he made good money from the sale of gravel from the land across from the Glebe. After his death, his son, Henry, took over the farm. He also rented Waterloo Farm from 1941, until he inherited it from John Dewar-Harrison in 1967. In 1966, he sold Glebe Farm to John Lawrence, a farmer, whose son, Richard, succeeded him. He converted the property and left in the mid-1980s, when he sold it to the Herrings. They have developed it as a camping and fishing site.

Glebe Farm, with Alfred Taylor, his wife, May, and son, Henry,1920s (Diana Joslin)

(d) The Laurels

As has been noted, in the 1990s, Richard Wise sold Laurels Farm in the village and built a new farmhouse, The Laurels, on the back road to Caversfield, where he now farms some 100 acres.

(e) Moat Farm (formerly Cotmore Farm)

Moat Farm, part of the Cotmore Estate, was owned by the Harrison family from 1815. At some point it was acquired by the Wyndham family of Caversfield and was occupied by their tenants. In 1851, it was occupied by Henry Barnes, labourer, and his family. By 1883, it was occupied by a bailiff, as it was in 1891, when William Berry was the bailiff, with his family, and Charles Spencer, a labourer, was a boarder. In 1901, Charles Spencer, a carter, was there with his wife, Henrietta (formerly Berry), and her son, Charles Berry, a butler, and a grandson. The Valuation Book of 1910 records Henry King of Waterloo Farm farming here with 125 acres and a further adjoining 62 acres owned by Mrs Augusta Dewar. The Mitchell family, who were shepherds, were living here in 1901 and 1911, and other shepherds followed them. At some point the Rigdens acquired the farm, and sold it to Norman Deeley some 30 years ago. He farms some 100 acres.

(f) Waterloo Farm

Soon after John Harrison purchased part of the Cotmore estate, 'he built a good farmhouse and buildings (probably on the site of one of the old cottages), and named it after the great victory, which was at that time the talk of every tongue, "Waterloo Farm".'[38] It was one of a number of farms built outside the village following the Enclosure Award of 1762. In 1851, John King was farming 515 acres with 23 labourers. In 1861, he was farming 520 acres, with 12 men, 4 boys and 3 girls. By 1871, his son, Henry, was only farming 230 acres with 6 men and 4 boys. The 1910 Valuation Book records him farming there with 224 acres, still as a tenant of Edward Slater-Harrison.

After Henry King's death in 1914, there was a series of tenant farmers until 1967, including Ernest Watts (by 1920) and Jonathan and William Allen in the 1930s. As has been noted, Henry Taylor rented Waterloo from 1941 until 1967, when he was gifted the farm by John Dewar-Harrison. After his death in 1997, his son, David, succeeded him. He is now the only large-scale farmer in the parish, farming some 1,800 acres with two helpers and some very large machinery. Recently he has built a large extension to the west end of the farmhouse.

(g) Kelly's

This property, opposite the Glebe, is a livery stable, run by John Kelly. His family had a livery stable for many years in the Southwold area of Bicester.

Fringford Mill

At the time of the Domesday Book (1086), there were two water mills in Fringford. The first one was near Poplar Spinney, not far from the small bridge. The second one was on the present site by the Buckingham road. The mill and surrounding fields were part of the 71 acres owned by Eton College at the time of enclosure in 1762. In 1913, the mill, mill cottage and other buildings, with some 9 acres, were occupied by W.Fenemore, who was leasing them from J.S.Mansfield, sub-tenant of Eton College. The Field Books give the following description: 'The stone & tiled cott cont'g 3 rms up, 2 down & Washroom, hovel & wall gdn. Mill, stable, Coachhouse & cattle shed. 2 pasture fields. Mill now used only occasionally.'

Shortly afterwards, Thomas Hanks Allen took over the Mill. Norah Morgan, his granddaughter, in an interview in 2007, recalled her grandfather and the Mill. 'My Grandfather.. bought the Mill in 1914 and there were about 10 acres with it then.' 'He used to do the grinding for almost all the farmers around here. They all knew Tommy Allen.' 'He used to do all the harvesting himself and he'd get casual labour to help him but he didn't employ anybody else as such except my father [Thomas Henry Allen].' 'I can remember being in the Mill and pulling on the cord sometimes to help to take the sacks up. You would put a *chain* round the top of the sack and then pull on the cord and it would take the sack straight up to the top of the mill and then it would be emptied into the hopper and it would go through to the next

Tommy Allen threshing at Waterloo Farm, 1930s. (Thomas Henry Allen)

Fringford Mill, cleaning party, 1930s. (Thomas Henry Allen)

Fringford Mill, cover picture for the sale brochure, 28 May, 1948. (David Watts)

Fringford Mill, sheep washing, 1930s. (Thomas Henry Allen)

storey down, it would go through the mill stones and be ground and then fall down to the hopper in the bottom.' 'The corn was threshed in sort of Octoberish and then people from then until about March, would send their stuff to be milled and then my father would leave the Mill and he was paid a retainer of 30 shillings a week for the summer and then when he came back again in September/October to take the threshing machine out again, he would then be paid £3 a week. But my grandfather only charged in 1946 when he retired, the same amount for the crushing and the grinding as when he went there in 1914. He never ever charged more and I've seen the booklet where he put it all down so I do know that's true! I think it was 3 *pence* a quarter they used to charge for crushing and 6 pence for grinding. I think that's what it was.'

She also described the sheep washing in the mill-stream: 'What they actually did, was to shut the top sluice down, bring all the water down here and then when it was sufficiently deep, they would open up the sluice and put a board across. There were two posts here. And they put a big board there and then they filled all of this part with water from the mill and when it was very deep, they could pop the sheep over the top and it was so deep that that they didn't break their legs you see when they dropped them in. They had long sticks because I can remember Mum saying she did it with someone from one of the nearby farms, to get the sheep to go underneath there and to run up the slope on the other side, and put them into other pens. They were just sheep washing, they weren't dipping.' The washing was *supervised* by a policeman to ensure that the sheep were not dipped for too long. The mill was sold in May 1948. The only other mill which operated in recent times was at Oldfields Farm, Stratton Audley and this ceased milling in the 1930s.

Fringford mill is still privately owned. Next door, Puratos, a Belgian company with its UK headquarters in Buckingham, now has an Innovation Centre, involved in research and training in the baking sector. After a thousand years of an active mill here, it is somehow appropriate to have a baking company on the site.

Summary

The number of labourers employed by all these farms show how labour intensive they were, at least in the 1850s and 1860s. There are further local examples, which show the high number of agricultural labourers employed in 1851: in Shelswell, William Sadler was farming 270 acres with 12 labourers; in Newton Purcell, Henry Foster was farming 317 acres with 14 labourers, and William Crawford 429 acres with 17 labourers; in Stoke Lyne, Samuel May was farming 850 acres with no less than 33 labourers. In Fringford, the number declined from 61 in 1851 to 34 in 1901. The 1860s saw a period of high farming with good employment prospects for labourers. This was followed by an agricultural depression from the mid-1870s to the mid-1880s, although 77 labourers are recorded in 1881. This figure, like that of 58 in 1891, seems high and it is likely that a number of them may not have been fully employed. There was another depression in the 1890s and by 1901 only 41% of those in work were employed in agriculture. By then, the population had declined from its nineteenth-century high of 479 to just 335 (see Chapter 7 with Tables 1-3).

Dairy farming was the norm in this area until the 1970s but arable and sheep farming are now predominant. Indeed, one of the farmers in neighbouring Hethe has some 4,000 sheep. The ledgers of the Price family (see Chapter 8), who had a good number of farmers as customers, confirm the local dominance of dairy farming in the late-Victorian and early-Edwardian periods. The twentieth century saw further decline in agricultural employment and the Twenty-Four Square Miles survey in 1943 (see Housing in Chapter 7) revealed that less than one-third of the population was then working on the land. Since then, there has been further serious decline and less than 2% of the working population now work on the land. In Fringford today, there are only four farms, Hall Farm, The Laurels, Moat Farm and Waterloo Farm, where David Taylor, with some 1,800 acres, is the largest.

Chapter 4 footnotes

[34] Blomfield, *Fringford*, 21.
[35] Letter from Kezia Whitton to her son, George, 14 November 1897.
[36] Blomfield, *Fringford,* 25.
[37] Blomfield, *Fringford*, 43.
[38] Blomfield, *Fringford*, 25.

Aerial photograph of Fringford, 1986. (Fringford School)

The Butchers Arms. (Peter Silver)

The Green with Laurels Farmhouse and Green Farm. (Paul Elliott)

Laurels Farmhouse. (Peter Silver)

Green Farm. (Peter Silver)

The Old School. (Peter Silver)

Hall Farm. (Peter Silver)

The Old Forge. (Peter Silver)

The Thatched Cottages. Lizzie Grantham's sweet shop was in the cottage to the right of them, next to Gable Cottage (now demolished), painted by Julie Barrett, 2006. (Julie Barrett).

Folly Cottages. (Peter Silver)

The Lodge. (Peter Silver)

The Whitton Gate to the Churchyard, c.1870. (Peter Silver)

Cast-iron cross marking grave of Zilpha Hinks, 1900. (Peter Silver)

Unveiling of the plaque to Flora Thompson by Linda Bassett (Queenie), 4 July, 2010. (Peter Silver)

Queenie (Linda Bassett) and Twister (Karl Johnson) in the BBC television series, 2008. (BBC Photo Library)

Rosemary Cottage, Church Lane. (Peter Silver)

Pringle Cottage, Rectory Lane. (Peter Silver)

Shelswell Park stable block after its restoration in 2000. (Baroness von Maltzahn)

The two sides of the Banner of the Mansfield Lodge of the Independent Order of
Oddfellows (Manchester Unity) No. 3904. (Fringford Village Hall)

Chapter 5

Church and Clergy

As has been noted, the earliest evidence yet found for a church at Fringford dates from 1103, although there may have been an earlier wooden building. Parts of the present stone church date from the early twelfth century. There is limited information about the early rectors but we do have a continuous list of names from 1565 (Appendix 4). The most interesting of them is John Bayley, a Presbyterian, who was made minister in 1645 during the Civil War. He replaced William Overton, who was ejected for refusing to accept the Act of Parliament abolishing the Book of Common Prayer. In 1648, Bayley, together with Samuel Wells, the Presbyterian Minister of Banbury, went to London to petition for the King's life. For his courage he was himself ejected but allowed to continue living in Fringford until the restoration of Charles II in 1660. He was then reappointed rector of Fringford and served as a loyal Anglican until 1697. He and his wife are both buried in Fringford.

From the middle of the eighteenth century to the end of the nineteenth century Fringford was particularly fortunate in its rectors.[39] The Revd John Russell Greenhill (1756-1813) was a cousin of the Russell family, who were descended from Oliver Cromwell. They owned Chequers in Buckinghamshire before it was given to the nation for the use of our Prime Ministers, and Greenhill himself had a large estate at Ellesborough, near Chequers. He was non-resident for the first ten years of his incumbency, staying at Croydon, and Charles Cotton was his curate at least from 1764-66. In 1767, he moved to Finmere, and from 1773 he lived in Cottisford, where he leased Cottisford House from Eton College. As he explained in a letter to Edward Palmer in 1776, 'The pleasant situation, & the clean country- to both which I am extremely partial, together with the neighbourhood to Fringford, which I have been rector of near 20 years (but had no house there I could profitably live in) tempted me to give a very extravagant Price [£7,300] for my purchase here [Cottisford House] three years ago.'[40] In 1779, he also became rector of Marsh Gibbon.

Although Greenhill never lived in Fringford, he took a great interest in it. Two of his manuscript diaries survive, in which he entered his daily engagements and recorded meticulous weather observations.[41] These and other records show him to have been very social but also unusually conscientious in a period when there were many absentee and pluralist parsons who never visited their parishes. The diaries also give the reader an interesting insight into the daily life of an eighteenth-century parson in the 1780s and 1790s.

For the next 80 years, from 1814 to 1894, the parish benefited enormously from the personal wealth, intellectual ability and social standing of three 'regal rectors': Henry Roundell, Henry de Salis and Cadwallader Coker. The church was largely rebuilt in this period. The attractions of such a small rural parish are not immediately obvious. However, the Crown had taken over the advowson (the right to present the rector) in 1766 and by 1817 the annual tithes and stipends were some £431. This was a good sum in those days and compares well, for example, with less than £120 received by the vicars of neighbouring Fritwell. The location of Fringford, close to Oxford and the Bishop, may also have been a bonus, since all three rectors were Oxford men. The Revd Henry Roundell (1814-52) came from a great Yorkshire family and was 'possessed of ample means and a genial temperament'. Apart from his major improvements to the Rectory, 'He was also responsible for the rebuilding of the chancel and much of the other restoration of the church. He also let out part of the glebe as allotments for the labourers, 'a rare kindness at the time.' 'Thus, in days of too common laxity, he was careful of his flock.'[42] In 1846, he became the first Rural Dean of the Bicester Deanery. In 1848, he was described by his churchwardens as very sober, his dress gentlemanly and becoming a minister, although Bishop Wilberforce found him 'a little huffish'! There seems to have been a genuine affection for him in the parish and when Wilberforce spoke at his funeral in 1852, there were 'many wet eyes'.[43]

The Revd Henry Fane de Salis (1852-73) was another rector of ample means. He came from a Swiss family and his great great grandfather was sent as envoy of the Graubinden (Grisons) to Queen Anne and was created Count of the Holy Roman Empire in 1748. Henry's great grandfather (the 2nd Count) was naturalised by Act of Parliament in 1730, marrying the Hon Mary Fane.[44] Henry was also son-in-law of J.W.Henley, who was a Cabinet Minister in the 1850s. He had been rector of Shalstone, near Buckingham, for nineteen years and Rural Dean of Buckingham. He completed the restoration of the church and built the new National School in 1866. He also added two cottages for labourers on Glebe Farm and increased the allotments.[45] He became Diocesan Inspector but resigned from Fringford in 1873 on succeeding to property at Portnall Park, near Virginia Water in Surrey. The Revd Cadwallader Coker (Mr Coulsdon in *Lark Rise*) (1873-94) was a member of a large and distinguished Bicester family, the owners of Bicester Hall. 'He was 'a clergyman of the old type' who 'preached to his poorer parishioners contentment with their divinely appointed lot in life and submission to the established order of earthly things.'[46] He and his wife both died in April 1894.

In 1894, democracy came to Fringford with a vengeance, with the arrival of the Revd Charles Thompson (Mr Delafield) (1894-98). He was married but did not have any children, although Flora Thompson gives him two daughters in *Lark Rise*; this gives her the freedom to discuss children in the community. However, her description of the new rector sounds very authentic. 'Dignity did not enter into his composition. He would run out to post a letter.. in his shirt-sleeves' and he had a

St Michael and All Angels Church, early 1900s. (Peter Morrall)

charming way of relieving any old woman of her load, like a faggot of sticks or a clothes-basket of washing. Some missed Mr Coulsdon 'He was a gentleman if ever there was one!' Others liked Mr Delafield because he was 'not proud and stuck up', and he soon won the 'reputation of being the best preacher in the neighbourhood – some said in the county.' As a parishioner was heard to say 'A sermon like that makes you feel two inches taller.' 'On summer Sunday evenings the church was often so well filled that late-comers had to stand in the aisle.' Oh that it could be so today! 'By the majority, judgement was suspended, "You've got to summer and winter a man before you can pretend to know him" was an old country maxim much quoted at the time.'[47] After he left Fringford in 1898, Thompson became vicar of Belgrave with Birstall in Leicestershire. In 1905, he was made Rector of Daventry and Rural Dean in 1906. He died in St Albans in 1916 aged 60.

Church attendance during the late eighteenth and nineteenth centuries seems to have compared favourably with that in other local churches. The Revd Greenhill found Fringford parishioners in general 'very good frequenters' of the church; he made a practice of counting them and found there were about 100 and more in the summer. This was impressive, given a population of only 252 in 1801. In 1768, when the unusually large number of 56 people wanted to be confirmed, he had visited every house and spoken widely on the subject. By 1808, when he was 77 years old and had a curate, he no longer read services, but he attended regularly and always visited the sick himself. In the 1851 Religious Census, estimated attendance was 130 in the morning and 200 in the afternoon, when the population was 357. The pattern of services was changing, particularly the number of communion services. In 1805, there were only six a year, by 1817 they were monthly but it was not until the 1890s that weekly communion was celebrated. There were also celebrations on Great Festivals and Holy Days after about 1850. Attendance was variable and it decreased significantly in the 1880s. In 1899, however, the rector described it as 'very satisfactory'.

In spite of a significant decline in attendance during the twentieth century, there was little change in the nineteenth-century pattern of services until the 1960s. Until the 1920s, most of the local parishes had their own resident parson, who was often a very powerful individual. Locally, there were a number of organisational changes in the ten Shelswell parishes well before the 1960s, partly due to the shortage of clergy. In 1924, Archdeacon Whylock Pendarvis became rector of Fringford and Hethe. In 1954, John Westlake became rector of Fringford, Hethe and Newton Purcell (1954-63). It is generally agreed locally that he was the first rector since Charles Thompson to provide a democratic leap forward. He is remembered fondly for his gift of getting on with everybody, playing the piano and singing in the pub, and making his own wines.

From 1968 to 1978, John Sergeant was rector of Newton Purcell, with responsibilities for Cottisford, Fringford, Hardwick-with-Tusmore and Hethe. In 1976, Anthony Hichens returned from missionary work in Guyana and was appointed priest-in-charge of Stratton Audley, Godington, Stoke Lyne and Finmere-with-Mixbury. In 1978, Donald Allan, who succeeded John Sergeant, was appointed priest-in-charge of Finmere with Mixbury, and together with Anthony Hichens looked after all ten parishes. Sorting out how the ten parishes were to be run resulted in arguments and correspondence covering nearly five years. The parish has always been a powerful unit, with a natural strength and independence. Even today, the parishes all know what services they like and are ready to demand a fair and equal share of the resources available. Agreement was finally reached in 1983, when the Shelswell Group Ministry was formed, followed later by the creation of the Shelswell Benefice.

The Shelswell Benefice.
On 1 March 1983, the Shelswell Group Ministry was formally established for religious purposes. At that stage it was divided into the Northern Benefice (Cottisford, Finmere-with-Mixbury, Hardwick-with-Tusmore, and Newton Purcell-with-Shelswell) under Donald Allan and the Southern Benefice (Fringford, Godington, Hethe, Stoke Lyne, and Stratton Audley) under Anthony Hichens. Ronald Jennison, who had been Rector of the Riviera, replaced Donald Allan six months later. He retired in 1992 and Warwick (Ricky) Yates was inducted in January 1993. On 1 December 1995, he became the first rector of the newly created ten-parish Benefice of Shelswell. In 2001, there were two formal mergers, between the parishes of Godington and Stratton Audley, and the parishes of Cottisford and Hardwick-with-Tusmore. On 13 August 2009, Christobel Hargraves succeeded Ricky Yates as

rector. She resigned and left the area in October 2014. Her successor, Alice Goodall, has just been appointed. With declining attendance and a shortage of clergy in the Shelswell Group, it is becoming increasingly difficult for the benefice to maintain and service ten churches and for all the parishes to pay their share to the Diocese. There is a vital need for a new strategy, which might well include more services taken by lay people and more of them held in private houses, like the Methodists in Lark Rise.

The church of St Michael and All Angels is much as it was in the days when Flora Thompson sat behind Mrs Slater-Harrison (Lady Adelaide) and 'admired the way she knelt for the prayers, not plumping down squarely with one boot-sole on each side of a substantial posterior, as most other women of her age did, but slanting gracefully forward with the sole of one dainty shoe in advance of the other. She was tall and thin and, Laura thought, aristocratic-looking.'[48] There is now a plaque to commemorate Flora's years in Fringford (1891-97) and an avenue of prunus trees and a plaque in the south porch in memory of Mr John Dewar-Harrison, Lady Adelaide's nephew. He died in 1967 and is remembered fondly by many local people, particularly those tenant farmers who were left their farms in his will in return for paying the related estate duty. Currently (2015), an application is being prepared for a grant towards a connection to water and sewage, the insertion of glazed screens between the arches dividing the north aisle from the nave, the creation of a new servery, and the partitioning of the vestry to include facilities for the disabled.

Nonconformists[49]

Fringford seems to have been loyal to the Church of England since its creation, with few instances of Catholics, Methodists or other Nonconformists in the village. In the late eighteenth century, there was a small group of Presbyterians, who were licensed to meet in the house of Daniel Mansfield. They died out in the early 1800s. As has been noted, the Fringford rectors were very caring of their congregation in the nineteenth century. They were also used to controlling their parishioners and were not inclined to be tolerant of the few Nonconformists or 'dissenters' who lived in the village. In 1817, Roundell commented on 'two young men of loose and idle habits who frequent, I am told, a small meeting house in Hethe'. In 1838 there were 'a few families of Wesleyan Methodists, no public place of worship'. Similarly in 1854, 'Dissent: no place. A few meet in a cottage – 3 families'[50]. These three were probably the Claydon, Cowley and Harris families. In the 1840s, the Wesleyans obtained licences to meet in the house of William Walker and later in those of Mrs Tame (or Thame) and Mrs Harris.[51] The 1841 census seems to show Harris and Thame families living in three adjoining houses. There are indications that some members of these families moved to the more open society of neighbouring Hethe, where various houses were licensed for Methodist meetings from 1794 and a chapel had been built by 1854. In 1832, Hethe also had a new Catholic church erected, one of the first to be built after the Catholic Emancipation Act of 1829.

Although the 1851 Religious Census records a service at an Independent chapel in Fringford, with a congregation of 63, there is no other evidence that there was ever a chapel in Fringford. It seems highly unlikely that there was ever such a gathering of Independents in the village, given the active discouragement of any dissent by Henry Roundell. The census figures, which were provided by Thomas Freeman, a local preacher from Launton, seem to be a simple mistake or mis-allocation.

Chapter 5 footnotes

[39] For this section, see also the author's *Parishes, Parsons and Persuasions, The Contrasting Clerics and Communities of Fringford and Fritwell in 19th- century North Oxfordshire* (1997, unpublished).

[40] Letter from the Revd John Russell Greenhill to Edward Palmer, 28 June 1776. It is a very detailed letter about the possible enclosure of the common fields of Cottisford, in which Palmer was closely involved. The attempt was unsuccessful, and the enclosure award was not made until 1854.

[41] Revd John Russell Greenhill, *Diaries 1780-87 and 1793-1800.*

[42] Blomfield, *Fringford,* 38-39.

[43] MS.Oxf.Dioc. c.278; d.550; d.178.

[44] I am indebted to Margaret Wilson of the de Salis family for this information.

[45] Blomfield, *Fringford,* 39.

[46] *Lark Rise,* 425.

[47] *Lark Rise,* 523-9.

[48] *Lark Rise,* 465.

[49] See also the author's *Pilgrim's Progress Revisited, The Nonconformists of Banburyshire 1662-2012* (Wychwood Press, 2013).

[50] MS.Oxf.Dioc. d 701.

[51] ibid. c 646, f 116; c 647, f.33.

Chapter 6

Schools and Education

'What do our young Alf want wi' a lot o' book larnin'?' they would say.
'He can read and write and add up as much money as he's ever
likely to get. What more do he want?'[52]

When Flora was growing up in the 1880s, a section of the people still resented their boys being kept in school when they might be earning. They could join their fathers on the land, aged eight or less, and make a useful contribution to the family budget. However, Forster's Education Act of 1870 provided that elementary schools should be established wherever school provision was insufficient. This was followed by further legislation in 1876 and 1880, which established that all children should receive elementary education and that school attendance to the age of ten was compulsory. Before we look at the effect of all this legislation, let us examine what schools and education had been available in Fringford before.

The Early Schools 1768-1902

As early as 1768, Dr Addington and the Revd John Russell Greenhill started a small school, teaching the catechism, reading and writing, in a house provided by Dr Addington. He and the rector paid the fees of twelve of the poorest children in the parish to attend the school. The teachers at the school (a brother and sister) were brought into the parish by Dr Addington, who also provided a house for them. By 1823, and probably earlier, there were Sunday schools for boys and girls. By 1834, there were three daily schools, with 20 boys and 16 girls between the ages of three and nine, supported by parents, Lord Sidmouth and the Revd Henry Roundell; also Sunday schools for boys and girls, supported by the rector. Other parishes do not seem to have been so fortunate, as Henry Roundell comments in 1838 that 'six places have no daily or Sunday school.'[53] It was his successor, the Revd Henry Fane de Salis, who made major changes immediately after his arrival in 1852. In 1853, he noted 'No school room. Half of the Old Tithe Barn fitted up by me as a School House for which purpose it now answers very well'. By 1854 there were 35 children here, and also an infant school for 20 and Sunday schools for 40 boys and girls. The tithe barn, which has been beautifully refurbished recently, is now part of Bancroft, next door to the Old Rectory.

It was also Henry de Salis who built the National (Church of England) School in

1866, on land leased from the squire, John Harrison Slater-Harrison, with places for 80 pupils. As previously stated, Kezia Whitton's two sons were among the first children to go to the new school. It was very unusual to go on to a Grammar School, as it was normal to leave school at the age of 12 and most of the Fringford pupils left then to go to work on the land. Henry de Salis also built the Old School House in 1876 on land leased from Lord Sidmouth. Edwin Blackburn and his wife, who were the first teachers in the National School, were the first occupants. After them all the teachers were female until the arrival of William Robinson in 1910. The 1910 Valuation records W.H.Robinson (head-teacher) occupying the 'Sch.mgrs house & garden'. He was a busy man, if perhaps not always a popular one, as he was assistant overseer, and assessor and collector of taxes for the parish.

Under Henry de Salis, there was also some education for parents who were interested. He started singing classes in the evening for them and in 1866 there were two evening classes. These seem to have been discontinued under the Revd Cadwallader Coker, although three of his daughters helped in the Sunday schools on a voluntary basis. Sunday schools continued under his successors and there were three or four voluntary teachers in 1899. There must also have been evening classes from time to time, because in 1911 the school managers were hoping that evening classes would be opened during the ensuing winter, which classes they thought were much needed in the parish.

1902-39

In 1902, the local authorities countrywide were given responsibility for elementary and secondary education. Although the old School Board was abolished and the school managers formed a new Education Committee, the school continued to be church-aided. The leaving age was now twelve, except for children in agriculture. Numbers on roll (NOR) continued to be about 60 and the minutes and logbooks do not indicate much in the way of change. In 1910, there was some concern when a teacher, Miss Blackshaw, announced her approaching marriage. Fortunately for her 'the Managers saw no reason to terminate her engagement on that account.' In 1911, the school closed early one day to see the hounds meeting at Fringford Bridge, as they were still doing in 1924 when the children attended the Bicester Hunt Meet on 11 November and the Silence was observed. There was continuing concern over the 'outside offices (i.e. the toilets), culminating in complaints from the District Inspector of Nuisances! There were some serious epidemics in this period and two children died of diphtheria in 1913.[54]

During the First World War there are very few references to the fighting in the logbook and the minutes. Gardening was added to the curriculum in 1914 and the subject was taken seriously with the need for extra food during wartime. The rector provided a plot in the Bridge Ground allotments near Fringford Bridge and in 1915 Arthur Jepson, the headmaster, passed the exam in Cottage and Allotment Gardening held by the Royal Horticultural Society. By 1917, food supply and

Schoolchildren in front of the Old Bake House, c.1910. (Price family)

distribution problems were exceptionally acute, because of the poor harvest of 1916 and the inability of the government to settle price inflation and prevent shortages. The contribution of school children therefore was vital but the curriculum and attendance could be a erratic in such an agricultural community. A late harvest, for example, could delay the start of school, as it did in September 1917 when the children were granted an additional week's holiday. They were needed to help their mothers with gleaning at the end of the harvest and the school managers had little hope of getting many pupils to school.

The potato harvest in September and October could have a similar effect, particularly in wartime, and there were school holidays of a week or more for the harvest during both World Wars. In September and October 1917 and 1918, the children were given a series of half-holidays to pick blackberries (to make jam) for the Army and Navy. As a result, in July 1917 the Government had to announce that allowances would be made for the marks lost by children employed in harvests after the holidays were over. There is no mention of the Armistice in November 1918 but we do hear of the National Holiday given for Peace Festivities on 18 July 1919. In 1918, the school leaving age was raised to fourteen.

In 1929, a fourth classroom was added, allowing the admission of children over 11 from six other schools, Cottisford, Finmere, Hethe, Mixbury, Newton Purcell and Stratton Audley. This enabled the NOR to increase from 60 to about 90. Bicester Grammar School had opened in 1924 but few children from Fringford achieved entry. In 1931, a fifth classroom ('the Hut') was erected at a cost of £125, mainly for practical work. This was not connected to the main building and there was an unfortunate accident early in the Second World War. One of the evacuees ran through the gap and was knocked down and killed by the lemonade lorry coming from 'Granny Wright's' shop on Rectory Lane. A steel railing was erected across the gap but it was not until 1960 that a new store was built between the main school and the hut, thus eliminating the dangerous gap. It is interesting to note some of the salaries paid to teachers before the Second World War: in 1916 Marie Lenore Miller, who later married Owen Judd, was taken on as an assistant teacher at £35 pa; in 1922, George Tolerton as Head at £320 pa; in 1929, Joe Ainley as Head at £229 pa and Winifred Harris as an assistant at £103 10s pa.

1939-73

In 1939, soon after the outbreak of war, a few evacuees started arriving from London by private arrangement. In June 1940, 62 children were admitted, including a party of 40 from the William McGuffie School in Walthamstow, which was formally admitted, accompanied by two teachers. This enlarged the school to five classes with 140 on roll. The NOR was fairly steady after this, although it rose to 159 by October 1940. This must have been a major disruption to the life of the school and the local residents who gave them homes. The logbook comments that the evacuees 'are constantly changing, some returning to their home towns and others being admitted, so that classes are by no means settled'. All except the last four returned in June 1945 and the NOR was back down to 90 by September 1945. A number of the evacuees have been contacted since then and it is interesting how varied their experiences could be. Some brothers and sisters were separated and some were very poorly treated. However, some flourished and enjoyed their stay and one even commented that he had been saved from a life of crime on the streets of Walthamstow! His hostess had been the formidable Mrs Smyly in Stratton Audley, who made sure that he behaved.

On 1 April 1942, Herbert Corfe took over as headmaster. He was exceptionally well qualified to come to Fringford. After 39 years in Tottenham and the headship of a large council school there, he led an evacuee party of 400 from Tottenham to the Fen District in September 1939 and organised their settlement. In June 1940, he led another party of evacuees to South Wales, where he became acting head of a large mixed school of some 300 evacuee children in Whitchurch, Cardiff. He left Fringford without notice on 18 May 1944, when his wife became seriously ill. He left an unusual headmaster's 'handover' letter to his successor, Len Standen.[55] A number of his comments about the school and the school house make amusing reading in our age of rather over-regulated education. They also show just how hard it was to cope with the influx of evacuees. The negative comments about the rector and his wife and the glowing comments about Ellen Price, the Postmistress, may also indicate how few people there were with whom he could talk comfortably. After his wide experience, he may have found Fringford rather unsophisticated and possibly unwelcoming. Here are some of his remarks.

'*managers won't interfere with you – tho' perhaps a Mr Cross – a youngish man from Finmere – might be inquisitive about Scripture.*'

'*Water: the pump in the scullery is useless and the water from it not fit to poison pigs. All the drinking water in buckets from the village pump – 50 yds.*'

'*Timetable – Nobody has bothered about a Timetable. I made out a complete one early on and it is somewhere in the desk in the "Hut"* [the old Playgroup building]. *It serves as timetable – used elastically. There are so many interruptions it is a practical impossibility to keep a timetable.*'

Mr and Mrs Standen and Mrs Wyatt (on right), late 1940s. (Judy Legg)

'*The Admission Register is not "up to date". The Summary register – I never made it up at all last year – its a farce.*'

'*Sch Milk Scheme: Mr Buckingham – across the Green – supplies* [from Hall Farm]. *Children bring milk across in morning. Two each week supervise distribution and clean bottles.*'

'*Rev Harrington & Mrs Harrington – the less said the better.*'

'*Mrs Price (Postmistress)* [Ellen] *is a most intelligent lady – delightful to talk to.*'

'*P.S. I believe you will like Fringford – it should serve your purpose well – its lovely country –you'll want for nothing – in a few years there will be great developments just the other side of Bicester – with new schools wanting headmasters. Get "dug" in for a year or two & keep your eyes open.*'

'*You can't spend money in Fringford. House rent £15 per annum - paid to the Rector. No school allotment now, we stopped it for good reasons.*'

How right he was about great developments and opportunities to come in Bicester, where the population in 1951 was only 4,171. The current major developments envisage today's population of some 40,000 doubling in the next ten years to more than 80,000. However, Len Standen stayed on as head until his retirement in 1963, and his wife continued her part-time teaching for a while after that. Len and his family had been evacuated from London to Wales. They moved to Fringford because their daughter Judy's education began to suffer with most of her lessons being given in Welsh. They had rented out their Wimbledon home and planned to return there after the War. However, under the current legislation, it was extremely difficult to evict sitting tenants. Len appealed directly to Parliament and Winston Churchill used the 'Standen Case' to tackle the plight of evacuated families

Old School, before the building was joined to the Hut. Note the railings put in the gap following the death of an evacuee, 1950s. (Judy Legg).

and amend the law relating to sitting tenants. Churchill's personal note of thanks to Len Standen has survived (see opposite), to provide Fringford with a tenuous link to the Great Man. Eventually, Wimbledon Council was given permission to buy the Standens' house and this enabled them to build Bancroft on Rectory Lane for their retirement. William James was acting head until James Woodworth was appointed head in 1964, with Mrs Branwen Woodworth as an assistant teacher.

In 1946, the leaving age was raised to 15. Attendance could still be erratic. In October 1946, for example, when food shortages and strict rationing still prevailed, there were again a large number of absentees for the potato harvest. In 1949, Fringford was reorganised as a Junior Central School, with ages 5-7 coming from Fringford and Godington, and ages 8-11 from Fringford, Hardwick, Hethe, Godington, Cotmore and Caversfield. There were now only three classes and the NOR dropped from about 90 to 60. Seniors now moved on to Bicester, where the new Highfield Secondary School was built off Queen's Avenue in 1952. In 1963, the Grammar School moved to the same site and in 1965 the two schools were amalgamated into Bicester School (subsequently Bicester Community College in September 1987). In 1951, owing to the increasing problems and costs of repairs and maintenance, the managers decided to hand Fringford school over to the Local Education Authority (LEA) and it became Church-controlled rather than Church-aided. Apart from the building of the canteen in 1952 and the new stores and 'offices.' in 1960, the Old School remained much the same until 1970. By then it was cramped for space, had no adjoining playing fields, and was riddled with mice. The Education

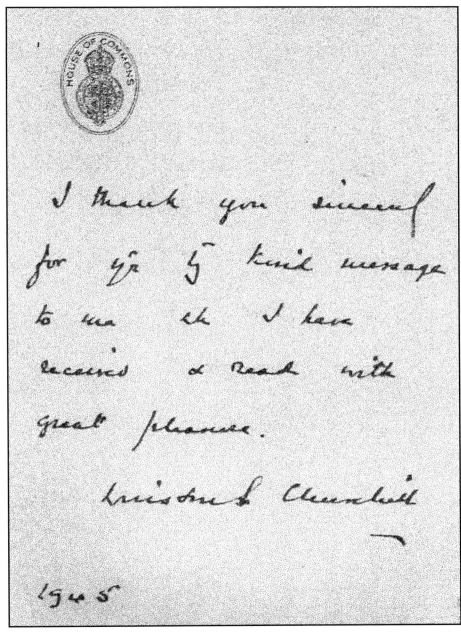

Churchill's note of thanks to Len Standen for bringing to his attention the problem of evicting tenants from the Standens' home in Wimbledon. Churchill used the 'Standen Case' to amend the law relating to sitting tenants. (Judy Legg)

I WISH TO MARK, BY THIS PERSONAL MESSAGE, my appreciation of the service you have rendered to your Country in 1939.

In the early days of the War you opened your door to strangers who were in need of shelter, & offered to share your home with them.

I know that to this unselfish task you have sacrificed much of your own comfort, & that it could not have been achieved without the loyal co-operation of all in your household.

By your sympathy you have earned the gratitude of those to whom you have shown hospitality, & by your readiness to serve you have helped the State in a work of great value —

Elizabeth R

Mrs. E. Hinks.

Evacuee certificate awarded to Emily Hinks, 1945/6. (Gladys Hinks)

Committee needed to make savings and it was decided to close the schools in Stratton Audley and Hethe and build a new larger school in Fringford.

Memories of Fringford School 1952-55[56]

Martin Mills, who was at Fringford School from 1952 to 1955, has recently written his memories of those school days, which have not been published but are a joy to read in his beautiful handwriting. They make fascinating reading, in particular his tributes to Mr Standen and his wife. He makes it immediately clear how grateful he is to him, 'a very gifted teacher. He managed to give children a thorough knowledge of the 3Rs whilst still maintaining a wide, rich curriculum – no mean feat in the 1950s.' You might well say the same of any teacher managing this in 2015. He joined the school in September 1952 in Mrs Standen's class and left in 1955, after passing the Eleven-Plus Exam; this allowed him to go to Bicester Grammar School rather than a secondary modern. The following quotes provide some interesting comments on school life at the time:

'There were four house teams –Wordsworth (green), Shakespeare (red), Milton (blue) and Scott (yellow). There were house points for good work and behaviour and we were highly motivated to put our team into the lead.'

'On Mondays there was money to be given in – 1 penny for school fund (by my final year enough had been raised to buy a slide projector), sixpence for a National Savings Stamp, and dinner money.'

'The school dinners were excellent, the hot puddings such as treacle sponge being especially delicious. Miss Hinks [Gladys Hinks who still lives in St Michael's Close] was the cook, helped by Mrs Powell [later the Postmistress] and Mrs Young.'

'Sometimes, at dinner time, we asked permission to go "round the alley' [Ghost Alley], a path leading past the church; en route, you could buy sweets at the village shop (probably 'Granny Wright's' in Prentice's Yard). At other times we could go beyond the green and watch the blacksmith at work [William Plumb at the Forge].'

'Mrs Standen was a lovely lady, kind and enthusiastic. Besides the 3Rs she taught us music, mainly through folk songs. She also loved "Wind in the Willows", which she read to us at the end of each school day.'

'In September 1953 I went up to Mr Len Standen's class in the hut. He expected us to work hard and behave well, and we did. He inspired respect; when a child behaved badly he could become angry. He was, though, sympathetic and a marvellous teacher, one of the very best I've come across in the whole of my life. He had the priceless quality of clarity; everything made perfect sense. Under him we achieved our full potential. When you consider that he was dealing solely with working-class children, the 11+ results for Fringford school were outstanding.'

'At the end of each day Mr Standen would read to us, something he did brilliantly. One book was 'Emil and the Detectives', which was also serialised by BBC Schools' Radio. At the end of term we could choose favourite extracts from books. These were invariably the packing of hampers scene from "Three Men in a Boat", and the bishop giving Jean Valjean his candlesticks – "Please, sir, can you read 'Lez Misrubbles'? [Les Miserables].

'PE lessons had to be outside as there was no room for them indoors; so in winter we didn't have PE at all. Mostly we went on to the green to play rounders, stoolball or cricket, and admire the horse chestnut tree (Sometimes, we had to drive Mr Wyatt's cows off the grass before we could start playing).'

In conclusion, he writes 'Fringford was a wonderful school which instilled good work habits and gave us an excellent grounding in the 3Rs, whilst not neglecting the wider curriculum.'

Oh that OFSTED would or could write such conclusions to their inspections today. Unsurprisingly, Martin Mills himself became a teacher and held three headships and acting headships in Surrey before he retired in 2000.

1973-2015

The new school opened on 12 September 1973, on the other side of the Green. The old school became a Victorian Study Centre and in the early 1980s 'the Hut' became home to the Shelswell Playgroup. The new school had 66 children on roll and a compliment of three and a half teachers, led by Mr and Mrs Woodworth. James Woodworth served as head until 1986, while Mrs Woodworth carried on until 1990. Mrs Shirley Armitage succeeded Mr Woodworth and, at the same time, Mrs Barbara Nowakowski was appointed part-time administrator and she is still in post. By then, the NOR was down to 33, almost the school's low point (29). In 1993, the Governors created another class and appointed Miss Michelle Mairs to teach Class 4. In 1996, Mrs Armitage retired and was succeeded by Anthony 'Tony' Instone. When he was appointed to the headship of King's Meadow Primary School in Bicester in 2000, he was succeeded by Mrs Susan Pearson. In 2003, the Playgroup relocated to a new building next to the school. In 2004, the old school site was sold and the school building converted to a superior private house. Conversion included the demolition of 'the Hut', which had managed to survive since 1931. The school continues to flourish with some 100 pupils, as does the Playgroup. Mrs Pearson retired in July 2015 and has been succeeded by Mr Franco Pastore.

Chapter 6 footnotes

[52] *Lark Rise*, 182.
[53] MS.Oxf.Dioc. b.41.
[54] Fringford School logbook, 1913.55 Letter from H.A.Corfe to J.L.Standen, 11 June 1944.
[56] Martin Mills, *Memories of Fringford School 1952-55* (2013/14, unpublished).

Chapter 7

Changes in Village Life

'Every member of the community knew his or her place and few
wished to change it.'[57]

Flora Thompson describes a very ordered community, in which 'those at the top had
no reason to wish for change and by others the social order was so generally accepted
that there was no sense of injustice.' In historian's terms, Fringford, like most of the
neighbouring villages, was 'closed' rather than 'open'. A closed village may be
described as one where a squire or absentee landlord owns at least half the acreage,
while an open village would have many small proprietors. As we have seen,
Fringford was very much under the control of the Slater-Harrison family of
Shelswell, and this was enhanced by the rector's holdings of glebe land. This control
may not exist today but there is still a very real consciousness of the Shelswell Estate.
In this chapter, I look at some of the major changes in village life since Flora's
Victorian childhood.

Population

The population figures for the Shelswell Group from 1801 to 2001 (Table 1), show
clearly how the population of Fringford declined from a nineteenth-century peak of
479 in 1871 to 335 in 1901. Most of the other villages also had their peak populations
between 1851 and 1871. The agricultural depression of 1874-84 brought an end to
the boom of the 1860s, and caused severe rural poverty. This was aggravated by a
second agricultural depression from 1891-99, partly caused by foreign competition,
with frozen meat coming in from Australia, New Zealand and South America. Even
in Lark Rise 'The Innkeeper's wife got in cases of tinned salmon and Australian
rabbit'.[58] These depressions contributed to large numbers moving to the towns or
emigrating. Between 1871 and 1911 six million Britons emigrated, with the peak in
the 1870s and 1890s. Most of the emigrants were men from rural areas, so that by
1900 there were over one million more women than men in Britain. Advertisements
in the *Bicester Advertiser* at the time included many offers of free land, in Canada,
New Zealand and Australia. By 1901, however, Canada was 'the only country
offering free land to home seekers of limited means.' No less than 50,000 per annum
were entering her ports. In many cases the parishes also gave some support to those
wishing to emigrate, as they had done earlier in the nineteenth century. There were
also 'assisted passages' provided for some emigrants.

By the late 1890s, men in the villages with any ambition were looking for wider

TABLE 1

Population in the Shelswell Group

Village		1801	1851	1871	1901	1931	1951	2011
Fringford		252	357	**479**	335	268	331	602
Cottisford	(Note 3)	106	263	**269**	175	139	154	216
Hardwick	(Notes 3&4)	61	66	74	46	37	113	
Tusmore	(Notes 3&4)	31	**52**	43	51	82		
Finmere		308	**399**	327	226	187	265	466
Hethe		262	418	393	311	293	288	275
Mixbury	(Note 5)	304	**402**	338	221	186	184	370
Newton Purcell		93	117	122	103	130	103	
Shelswell	(Note 6)	42	43	43	45			
Stoke Lyne	(Note7)	334	**631**	603	409	381	231	218
Stratton Audley		**379**	305	368	270	327	306	434
Godington	(Note 8)	99	87	70	57	60	45	
Total		2,271	2,696	2,580	1,857	2,090	2,020	2,581
Town								
Banbury		4,070	8,793	11,768	**13,026**	13,998	18,916	46,525
Bicester		1,946	3,054	3,328	3,023	3,110	4,171	32,642
Oxford		12,279	27,843	31,404	**49,386**	80,539	98,684	151,900
Oxfordshire	(Note 9)	111,977	170,434	177,960	181,149	209,784	275,808	653,800

Notes

1. **Bold type** = peak population 1801-1901
2. Figures are no longer available for the smaller parishes, for confidentiality reasons.
3. In 2001, there was a merger of the parishes of Cottisford and Hardwick-with-Tusmore.
4. Hardwick and Tusmore were combined as a civil parish in 1932.
5. In 2011 Mixbury includes Newton Purcell with Shelswell.
6. Shelswell was combined with Newton Purcell in 1911.
7. In 1948 Fewcott was transferred from Stoke Lyne to Ardley parish.
8. In 2001, there was a merger of the parishes of Godington and Stratto Audley.
9. The large increase in the population of Oxfordshire by 2011 is partly accounted for by the merger with Berkshire in 1974.

opportunities in factories, on the railways and docks, and in the new urban police forces. Kezia Whitton has an interesting comment in November 1897, when she must have been looking for a young man to work at the Forge: 'I havent heard of anyone yet as there is nobody about as young men wont do it there is constantly 3 or 4 wanted in the Oxford times every week- I sent an Advertisement to the Northampton Herald a fortnight ago last Saturday but have only had 2 answers which were of no use.' There was also growing competition from mass-produced goods and declining local markets, which affected, for example, bootmakers, blacksmiths, tailors and wheelwrights, and also women's employment, as we shall see below. By 1901, 'the aggregate number of male farm labourers, shepherds and farm servants employed at all ages in England and Wales had fallen from over 920,000 in 1871 to just over 600,000.'[59] In the twentieth century, there was further decline in the population of Fringford, particularly after the Great War, and it did not return to its 1901 level until 1951. At that point, the local community still remained close-knit and mainly self-sufficient, with its own shops, craftsmen and tradesmen. New housing developments, starting in the 1950s, have seen a steady rise in the population, which has now doubled to over 600 (see Housing below).

Emigration- The Butler Family[60]
As noted above, the peak in emigration was in the 1870s and 1890s, mainly to Canada, New Zealand and Australia. Nationally, the bare statistics are impressive enough, with six million Britons emigrating between 1871 and 1911, and most of the emigrants were men from rural areas. At a local level, emigration was clearly a topic for discussion, both in Juniper and Fringford. In Juniper, some relatives of Emma Timms, Flora's mother, who had settled in New South Wales and were on a visit to England, 'nearly persuaded Nurse Emma to go back with them.' Indeed, it was all settled until, one night, they began to talk about snakes and Emma changed her mind 'I shan't go, for I can't abear [sic] the horrid creatures.' But 'of the next generation her own second son [Frank] became a fruit farmer in Queensland and of the next a son of Laura's [Henry Basil] is now an engineer in Brisbane.'[61]

The personal experiences of a Fringford family, the Butlers, shed some interesting light on emigration. Henry Butler and three of his brothers emigrated to Australia, starting in 1869. Their story illustrates both the trials and the rewards for those prepared to try it, and why it could be preferable to working in England in this period. The Butler family's initial link with Australia came earlier, as 'John Butler and his eldest son, Reuben (born 1802), were tried for attempting to steal Chaff, were sentenced to death, but instead transported to Australia in 1827 on the *Prince Regent*.' John's nephew, Richard, was a cordwainer (shoemaker) in Fringford, married to Rhoda (Thame). They had 12 children, of whom four died in infancy and four sons emigrated to Australia, Henry, Joseph, Charles and Thomas. As we have seen, their sister, Sarah Butler Rennison (1850-1933), was the letter-carrier, and Richard's older brother, Patric [sic], was the local carrier (see Country carriers below).

Joseph (1848-1909) was the first brother to emigrate, sailing from Gravesend on the *Royal Dane* on 9 December 1869, and landing at Rockhampton, North Queensland. It seems likely that he had left Fringford earlier to join his brother, Henry, in Liverpool working on the railway. The 1860s saw some 2% of Britain's population emigrate to New South Wales, to which Queensland then belonged, and the brothers were probably attracted to the idea by stories circulating in Liverpool, the Gateway to the Empire. No doubt, Joseph, as the unmarried brother, agreed to emigrate first and pave the way for Henry and his family to follow, if he was happy with his experience - this was a common practice. His first job in Australia was as an engine driver in Brisbane, presumably based on his experience in Liverpool. His varied career then included panning for gold in North Queensland, and then spells with his brothers on Magnetic Island and in Townsville (see map). In 1900, he moved to Murray Upper, where he managed the 'Fringford' property for Thomas (see below).

Henry (1834-1924) had moved from Fringford to Liverpool in the late 1850s, where he worked on the railway. As we have seen, he must have been convinced by Joseph to join him in Australia. He and his wife, Elizabeth, with four young children, sailed from London (Gravesend) on 30 July 1870 on the *Royal Dane* (like Joseph) arriving at Rockhampton, Queensland, on 19 November 1870, only the 4th ship under the Immigration Act of 1869. They were due to go to Brisbane, but the Government of New South Wales ordered the ship and immigrants further north to Rockhampton to increase the settlement there. There was little work available there, so they moved further north to Mackay. After two years there, they moved to Townsville, where Henry was employed erecting fences round the Queen's Botanical Gardens. He also worked on road mending, before joining a gang employed to dig coral from the reef encircling Magnetic Island (opposite Townsville). The coral was brought to Townsville and pulverised to obtain lime for mortar, which was used for building the Townsville Court House. He purchased a small sailing boat and would sail to Magnetic Island on weekends, where he built a 'log and slab hut with a thatched roof' and was the first white settler among the local aborigines.

Charles (1852-1946) sailed from London on 25 July 1874 on the *Darling Downs* and arrived in Brisbane on 5 November 1874, closely followed by <u>Thomas (1856-1948)</u>, who sailed from London on 13 September 1874 on board the *Indus*, arriving in Brisbane on 29 December 1874; they were both on 'assisted passages'. The brothers then joined Henry on Magnetic Island, and 'erected a lime kiln, where they burnt coral and later freighted it in it's powered [powdered] form in their sailing boat to Townsville. Also from this they built their own coral house which was still in existence in 1938.' In 1877, Henry brought his family there, where they lived for 21 years. He died in 1924 but his daughter, Ellen, continued to live on Magnetic Island until her death in 1958.

Thomas left Magnetic Island and moved further north to Mackay to work as a line repair man and in 1896 he was transferred to the post office in Cardwell. In 1900,

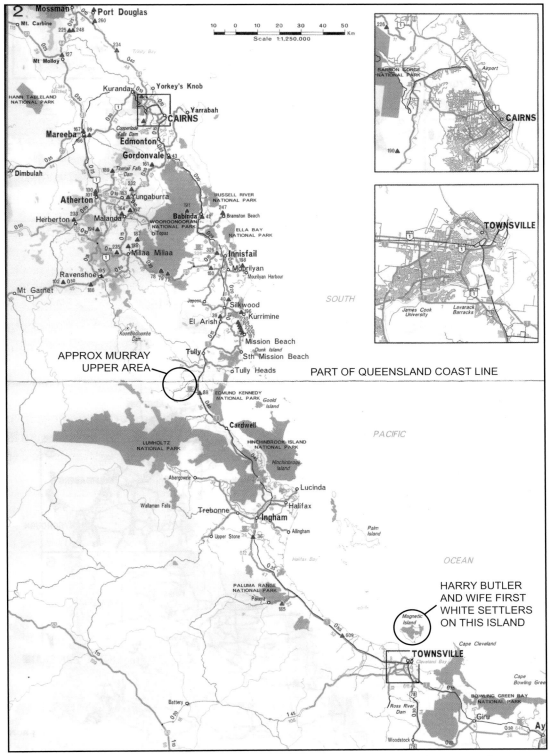

Map of North Queensland, Australia, showing Magnetic Island and Murray Upper, site of 'Fringford' Farm (marked by Grace Rutherford).

'Fringford' Farm, Murray Upper, North Queensland, 1920s. (Rhonda Smith)

Thomas, Henry and Charles Butler on Magnetic Island, North Queensland, 1920s.
(Rhonda Smith).

he purchased some 168 acres, of land, house and fruit trees in Murray Upper (the upper reaches of the Murray River). The property was then called 'Blechynden' which Thomas changed to 'Fringford'. Bletchingdon is another village in Oxfordshire, not far from Fringford, so it is possible that Leopold Stamp, who had built the house in the 1880s, may also have been an Oxfordshire man. As we have seen, Joseph moved to Murray Upper in 1900. He and his wife, Emma, managed the property until Thomas and his family moved there from Cardwell about 1902. Joseph then bought a property across the creek from 'Fringford', where he built a house called Gabbon and farmed the land and bred cattle and horses until his death in 1909.[62] Emma continued with the farm, although the house was destroyed by fire in 1914, but another house was built, called Gabbon II.

At the 'Fringford' farm, Thomas grew maize and bananas, raised fowls and pigs, and bred cattle and horses. All the produce was taken by horse-wagon to Cardwell for shipment to southern Australia, and they collected their groceries on the return trip. The whole trip took two or three days and at night they camped out on the side of the road. In 1926, Thomas took up post office work again, on the Murray River, and his son, Ormand, began the first motorised Royal Mail Service with a Model T Ford truck. Thomas lived on at 'Fringford' until his death in 1948. Electricity was not connected to the Murray District and 'Fringford' until 1974. None of Thomas' children married and like him they were all buried on the property, except for Hugh Ramsey, who was killed in action in France on 28 November 1916 while rescuing a friend.

The 'Fringford' log and slab hut was occupied until the last member of the family, Mts Shirley Butler, died in 1976. She was befriended by a fellow called John Ryan, who inherited 'Fringford' and he stripped it bare. He then sold it to the man who was running a historical village centre called Banana Land in Cardwell. The project was a failure and subsequently 'Fringford' and the centre all burnt to the ground. [63]

So there was a sad end to 'Fringford' but the Butler brothers with their families certainly played their part in the history of the early pioneers. Although it was a simple but hard life for them, three of the brothers seem to have prospered. Little is known of Charles, who seems to have been the 'black sheep' of the family. He never married and seems to have sponged off the brothers in turn. Family legend has it that Thomas's wife, May, once hunted him from the Fringford farm with a gun! It is worth noting how long-lived the family were, apart from Joseph who was only 61 when he died of tuberculosis, Henry (90), Thomas (92), Charles (94) and Sarah (82). The emigration experience had its challenges for the brothers but they were welcomed as immigrants, encouraged to buy land in areas which had never been developed, and they were their own masters. It was all a far cry from working in England in the 1870s, on the railway or on the land, for very modest wages of some 11s (55p) or 12s (60p) a week. It is very unlikely that they, except perhaps for Charles, had any regrets at their decision to emigrate.

Influence of the Great Houses

The Lark Rise people 'took a pride in their rich and powerful country-house neighbours, especially when titled,' and 'by some inherited instinct they felt that he [the Earl of Effingham at Tusmore] belonged to them.'[64] It was all a far cry from today's attacks on the wealthy. There are a number of large country houses in Lark Rise country, including Shelswell Park, Swift's House and Tusmore Park, although none of them is strictly a 'great house', like Blenheim or Stowe. They have been large enough to have their own supporting communities, while still being dependent on the local villages for a variety of services. In the next chapter, we see how widely the services of the Price family were needed as plumbers and decorators, particularly by the great houses like Shelswell and Tusmore.

The census returns provide an interesting picture of the households at these great houses. At Shelswell Park (Table 2) in 1861, the Slater-Harrisons had ten domestic servants (five born locally) and seven outdoor staff (all local). There were similar numbers from 1871 to 1911, apart from 1891, when they were away and left a 'skeleton staff' of 12 (five indoor, seven outdoor). In 1871, only two of the domestic servants were born locally, while six of the seven outdoor staff were local. The figures were very similar in 1881 and 1901. At Swift's House in 1851, only four of 17 staff were born locally. The Peytons, who were away in 1861 and 1871, had 19 staff in 1881, of whom nine were born locally. There were similar numbers in 1891 and 1901, of whom only a third were born locally.

The Bicester and Whaddon Hunt played a significant role on the local scene (see below), so it is worth noting that the Peytons' staff in 1901 included a coachman, a stud groom and four other grooms. At Tusmore Park in 1861 there were 18 domestic servants and 12 outdoor staff. By any standards this was an impressive household and much grander than Shelswell Park or Swift's House. None of the domestic staff were born locally and only four of the outdoor staff. By 1871, there were 20 domestic servants, of whom only two were local and 12 outdoor staff, of whom only four were local. The Earls were not in residence in 1881 and 1891. By 1901, the bachelor 4th Earl was in residence with four domestic servants (three local) and ten outdoor staff (three local).

The limited number of local domestic staff is part of a recognised pattern, with the gentry often employing most of their indoor staff from further afield. The diary of the Revd W.C.Risley, vicar of Deddington (1836-48), sheds some interesting light on the possible reasons for this. He rejected a candidate for the post of footman purely on the grounds that he had 'friends in the Place.' Similarly, a former servant from the Ewelme area of Oxfordshire recalled that it was usual for youngsters in her parish to be sent at least twenty miles away from home – 'probably to discourage followers or to stop the girls running home.'[65] By contrast, if you look at the households of the Fringford farmers, for example Cotmore and Waterloo, many of their servants were recruited from the local villages. However, if you were ambitious, the great houses provided much greater scope for advancement. That said, sooner

TABLE 2

Shelswell Park Domestic and Outdoor Staff 1861-1911

Year	1861	1871	1881	1891	1901	1911
				(Note 2)		
Domestic Staff						
housekeeper	1	1	1		1	
cook					1	1
lady's maid	2	1	1	1	2	2
house maid	2	2	2	2	3	3
kitchen maid	2	1	1	1	1	1
scullery maid		1	1	1	1	1
nurse maid		2				1
man nurse						1
butler	1	1	1			
footman	1	1	2		2	2
houseboy	1	1				
	10	11	9	5	11	12
Outdoor Staff						
stableman/groom	1			2	3	1
coachman					1	
gardener	1	1	1	1	1	3
gamekeeper	1	1	1	1	1	1
farmer	2	2	2	2	2	
shepherd	1		1			
land agent	1		1			
blacksmith		1				
ag.lab.		2	2	1	1	1
	7	7	8	7	9	6
Total Staff	17	18	17	12	20	18
Total Community	44	43	42	17	45	29
Notes						
1. In 1851, there were 18 staff, 13 domestic & 5 outdoor. Of the former, only the governess was titled.Total community was 43.						
2. In 1891, the Slater-Harrisons were away.						

TABLE 3

Trades and Occupations in Fringford 1851-1911

Male occupations	1851	1861	1871	1881	1891	1901	1911
Agricultural							
Farmer	7	7	6	5	7	7	7
agric. machinist				2	2		
blacksmith/farrier	1	3	5	3	4	4	5
carter		1		2	6	6	6
cattleman					2	3	2
farm bailiff	1	2	3	2	5	2	2
farm servant	6	2	3	3	4		
hurdle maker		1	1		1	1	
labourer	61	65	62	77	58	34	35
miller	2	1	1	2	2	1	1
ploughboy			1		1		
shepherd	1	4	6	2	5	7	7
timber haller (sic)			1		1		
wheelwright					2		
woodman					1		
Total agricultural	79	86	89	98	101	65	65
% of total occupat'ns	64%	60%	50%	51%	57%	41%	41%
Tradesmen							
baker	2	2	4	5	2	4	3
boot/shoemaker		5	7	2	1	1	1
cordwainer	6	3					
bricklayer/builder			1		1	4	3
brickmaker		1	3	2	3	2	
butcher		1	1	2	1	2	2
carman						1	2
carpenter	3	6	10	4	3	5	
carriage mfr	1						
carrier/assistants	2	1	1	1	3	2	2
coal haulier					1	1	
draper's assistants	1						
engine driver			1				
engineer/collector						1	1
fancy poulterer						1	
grocer/shopkeeper	2	1	1	1	2	1	1
ironmonger						1	
maltster/brewer	1	1	1	2	2	1	1
painter/plumber		2	3	2	3	2	2
roadman/contractor	1					1	2
sawyer			2		3		
soldier					1	1	
stonemason	2	4	4	1	1	1	
	21	27	39	22	27	32	20

	1851	1861	1871	1881	1891	1901	1911
Tradesmen (cont)	21	27	39	22	27	32	20
tailor	2	2	2				
wood carver						1	
Total tradesmen	23	29	41	22	27	33	20
Other occupations							
butler				1		2	1
chauffeur							2
coachman			2	2	2	1	2
errand boy	1						1
footman				1	2	1	2
gardener	1	1	2	5	6	10	11
gatek'pr/toll collector	1						
groom		2	3	3	2	5	11
postmaster/assistant					2	1	1
publican	1	1	1	1	1	1	1
rector/clergyman	1	1	1	2	1	2	1
schoolmaster				1		1	1
tram labourer							2
Total other occupat'ns	5	5	10	15	16	24	36
Total male occupat'ns	107	120	140	135	144	122	121
% of total occupat'ns	86%	84%	79%	71%	82%	76%	76%
Female occupations							
charwoman				2	1		1
dairymaid		1					
dressmaker/seamstress		4	1	8	4	1	1
domestic servant	9	11	28	33	13	19	28
fieldwoman	1	1		2	1		
governess				2			
housekeeper	2	1		3	4	10	4
lacemaker			5	2			
lady companion						1	
laundress	2			1	2	3	1
letter carrier					1	1	1
mid-wife/nurse				1	1		
school mistress	1	3	3	3	3	2	1
shopkeeper/grocer	1	1			1	1	1
victualler	1						
Total female occup'ns	17	22	38	55	31	38	38
% of total occupat'ns	14%	16%	21%	29%	18%	24%	24%
Total occupations	124	142	178	190	175	160	159
% of population	34%	35%	37%	46%	43%	48%	42%
Total Population	357	401	479	411	403	335	374

or later most youngsters from the country districts, particularly the girls, would have to move away to the towns, since it was here (especially in London) that the bulk of the vacancies for servants lay. The end of the nineteenth century also saw the growing reluctance of girls to enter service and the emergence of 'servant shortages', which 'became a menace' according to one member of the upper class![66]

In the twentieth century, the size of the estates and households reduced, particularly during and after the Great War. However, the need for indoor and outdoor servants continued both for them and the local farmers, even if there may now have been more emphasis on daily help from the local villages. The great houses also still needed help to run and maintain their estates, so that they continued to provide work for local tradesmen, including plumbers like the Prices, builders, electricians, butchers, and for other services and suppliers. All the Shelswell villages would have benefited, and indeed still benefit to a lesser extent, from this patronage, as do the local towns, Bicester, Banbury and Brackley.

As we see below, the great houses helped local employment by their support of the Bicester Hunt, and their influence extended to housing, which they provided for staff at Shelswell, Swift's House and Tusmore; in Fringford too, where John Dewar-Harrison converted the Manor in 1948 into houses for some of his workers on the Shelswell estate. It had proved impossible to build new houses for them because of shortages of materials after the war. The great houses have also owned most of the local farms, which have been worked by tenant farmers. As we have seen, John Dewar-Harrison showed his generosity by leaving his farms to the tenants, provided they paid their share of the estate duty.

Trades and Occupations

We have already seen (Chapter 4) the number and extent of the local farms since 1851, and the decline in the number of agricultural labourers with the rise of mechanisation. Table 3 shows how dependent the people of Fringford were on agriculture in the nineteenth and early twentieth centuries, as they were in all the Shelswell villages. If you include all those employed in occupations related to agriculture, the percentage declined from 64% of all males over ten in the village in 1851 to 50% in 1871, when the population was at its peak of 479. There was further decline, after the agricultural depressions, to 41% by 1901. The major decline was in the number of agricultural labourers. The figures of 77 in 1881 and 58 in 1891 seem very high and a good percentage of them were probably only working part time. 34 labourers in 1901 seems more realistic. The Table does show how the overall per-centage of those employed increased from 34% in 1851 to 48% in 1901, with a greater number employed in trades and other occupations. The year 1911 saw a temporary rise in the population to 374 but a decline in the percentage employed to 42%.

A number of trades are discussed elsewhere, for example, the Whittons at the Forge, the Mansfields' grocery store and the Prices' plumbing and painting business.

The Old Forge, with John and Kezia Whitton standing by the cart. William Eldefield, the watchmender, is standing on far left with a sledgehammer on his shoulder. Frederick Plumb is third from left, Zilpha Hinks stands in the doorway, late 1880s. (Bill Plumb)

One other local business was short-lived but deserves a mention, the Brick, Tile, and Drainpipe Works on Fringford Hill (formerly known as Brickyard Hill). The 1881 25" Ordnance Survey Map shows it, and also the Old Clay Pit, the Clay Mill and the Kiln. There was one brickmaker in Fringford in 1861 but the business seems to have taken off in the 1870s, with Thomas Foxley, the 1880s with William Carter and lastly William White, recorded in 1891 with his brother, and nephew, Albert. In 1901, William was Brickyard manager, with his nephew, Albert (23) as brick maker. By 1895, John Ward Smith was 'brick & pipe manufacturer on Sheep Street, Bicester.' In 1910 he is still recorded as 'brick, tile and lime manufacturer on Frinkford [sic] Hill' but there is no further mention of him, the Whites or the brickworks. Albert's

Kezia Whitton with Frederick Plumb, late 1890s. (Bill Plumb)

daughter, Dorothy Sparrow, says that he left after the clay ran out in about 1910. The Stratton Audley Road used to be called Clay Lane, after the Clay Pits, and there were also some sheds in the field called the Clays

Dorothy also says that her grandmother used to walk with a baby in the pram down to the Works at 5 every morning, with a hot breakfast of ham and eggs for the men, who had been burning the bricks all night. Tramps used to bed down near the kiln to keep warm. She thinks that the bricks may have been used for building work at Stratton Audley Park, after Major (later Lt Col.) George Gosling bought it from George Glen in 1891. They must have been used at a number of houses in Fringford, possibly including the Manor, after the Chinnerys arrived in 1898, and for Rosemary Cottage and Church Cottages. Bill Plumb says that they were used at the Forge, but were very poor quality and leaked.

After the Great War, jobs were scarce and many men had to travel further afield to find employment. Some cycled to London on a Monday and back on a Friday, while others cycled as far as places like Coventry. Not as alarming as it sounds, as there was comparatively little traffic on the roads then and the M40 was a distant dream. Jobs may have been scarce but Kelly's trade directories in the 1920s and 1930s show that the village retained many of the old trades and occupations. These included a butcher, a baker, two blacksmiths, plumbers, two or three shops, and the miller, and William Grantham was coalman for most of the period, but the last shoemaker, George 'Snobby' Judd, died in 1935.

It was a different story after the Second World War. As the number of horses on the land declined, to be replaced by tractors, blacksmiths turned their skills to repairing agricultural machinery and cars. At the forge, William Plumb had a gift for repairing any type of machinery. Similarly, coachmen adapted to become chauffeurs and mechanics, like Billy Judd, chauffeur to the Chinnery family, and stables were converted to garages. Boot and shoemakers suffered from the competition from Northampton and no one replaced Snobby Judd. Other trades were similarly affected by the rise in mass-produced goods, declining local markets and the growth of super-stores, such as Tesco.

Wages and Standard of Living

As Flora Thompson showed, life was hard in Lark Rise (Juniper Hill) and elsewhere in the late Victorian era, particularly for the labourers. A few years later, Lloyd George said 'low wages provided an existence not a life'. But Flora painted a rosier picture, 'After the Jubilee [Queen Victoria's Golden Jubilee of 1887] nothing ever seemed quite the same.' 'A change of farmers saw the introduction of 'the new self-binding reaping machine and women were no longer required in the harvest field.' 'Wages rose, prices soared, and new needs multiplied.'[67] 'Then about that time, came a rise in wages. Agricultural workers were given fifteen (75p) instead of ten or twelve shillings (60p) a week, and skilled craftsmen were paid an agreed rate per hour, instead of the former wage, irrespective of the time put in.'[68] As we have seen above, this was not enough to prevent mass migration from the villages to the towns and emigration to the colonies, like Canada, Australia and New Zealand.

The provision of allotments in many villages during the nineteenth century was a significant benefit for the poor, allowing them to live off their own produce. In Fringford, the Revd Henry Roundell (1814-52) 'commenced the plan of letting small allotments of land to the labourers of the parish, devoting some glebe to that purpose, a rare kindness at that time [1830s].'However, the most significant contributor to the labourers' menu was the family pig, which was 'everybody's pride and everybody's business.' 'During its life time the pig was an important member of the family, and its health and condition were regularly reported in letters to children away from home, together with news of their brothers and sisters. Men callers on Sunday afternoons came, not to see the family, but the pig.' After the killing by the pig-sticker, 'It was a busy time, but a happy one, with the larder full and something over to give away, and all the pride and importance of owning such riches.'[69]

The same would have been the case in Fringford, although there might have been less real poverty. The first decade of the twentieth century was a good one for the farmers, with the first rise in men employed on the farms since the 1860s. However, wages did not rise as much as prices and labourers were not as well off as, for example, casual dockers. It took until 1914 for a landmark agreement to be achieved at Sandringham, with 'The King's Pay and The King's Conditions', which included sixteen shillings per week (80p), a Saturday half-holiday and six-month tenancies for cottages. This may not have come into place elsewhere immediately but it did set a benchmark. After the Great War, times were hard and in the 1920s and 1930s jobs were scarce, and wages increased slowly. By 1935, the average weekly wage for men was only £2 16s 7d (£2.83) and for women £1 7s 3d (£1.36). On the cost side, however, a pint of beer was 7d (3p), 6 eggs 1s (5p), and a gallon of petrol, for the few who had cars, 1s 6d (1.75p litre). Even by the late 1950s, £5 per week was still an acceptable salary in London for an articled clerk in the legal or accountancy profession, when you could only dream of earning £5,000 pa. The explosion in salaries and wages was to come later.

The BBC started broadcasting in 1922 and most people bought wirelesses. In the absence of electricity in the homes, these were run off accumulators. Children used to take these over to Tommy Allen's shop in Hethe or to Billy Judd in Rectory Lane to be re-charged. Television did not make its appearance until the 1950s and it was a long time before it was generally affordable. The telephone was not in general use until after the Second World War, although the Stratton Audley Exchange was set up in 1927. There were only 14 subscribers, with Mrs Marion Chinnery at The Manor the only one from Fringford. Kelly's Directory of 1939 is the first edition to mention telephone numbers in the village. It records Cecil Cross, the butcher, as Stratton Audley 23 and Ernest Price at the post office as 20 – a far cry from today's six-figure numbers. Most people had to use the telephone kiosk outside the post office at

Pringle Cottage. At this stage, there was no direct dialling and all numbers had to be obtained through the local exchange. This gave the postmistress scope to listen to all the telephone calls, so villagers had to be careful what they said! An automatic exchange did not come in until about 1960. Today, of course, almost everyone has a mobile phone and a computer, even if rural reception can still be very poor.

Women's employment

'It was often the women who felt most keenly the attraction of a new life in the towns. As they started to go into towns for their shopping on a Saturday so they became more aware of the different, more exciting existence that awaited them there.'[70] By the end of the nineteenth century, many of the old country occupations, which had kept women busy and provided additional income, had gone or were in serious decline. The growth of mass-produced goods, like gloves (Worcester), lace (Nottingham), and stockings (Leicester), sounded the death-knell for these cottage industries. In 1851, the census records only 17 women, or 14% of the Fringford's working population, in employment. These numbers increased significantly in 1871 to 38 and to a peak of 55 in 1881; this was entirely due to the large number of domestic servants, 28 and 33. In 1901 and 1911, the overall figures were 38, or 24% of the village's working population. In 1900 nationally, 35% of all women over 15 were in paid employment but only 10% of married women. There was a general feeling that the place of married women was in the home. Mary Richardson, for example, whose son was killed in the First World War, did not continue teaching at Fringford School after she got married in 1892. In 1910, as previously noted, Miss Blackshaw had to have approval from the School Managers to continue teaching, after she announced her approaching marriage.

In towns, the early 1900s saw many new jobs for women. 'An Englishman, who had lived abroad continuously from 1874 to 1904 with only one short visit in 1888, was astonished at what he found on his return.' He remembered when 'the only lines of employment open to girls or women were; teaching, assisting in a shop, dress-making, or bar-keeping.' The new jobs included typists, telephone operators, physicians, bookkeepers, civil servants, and a variety of jobs in the post office. There were also the new ABC Refreshment Rooms, mainly in London: 'Sixteen years ago [1888] [they] were in their infancy. Now they are counted by the hundred, each with a staff of from ten to fifteen girls.'[71] In the villages, the main jobs were still limited to domestic service, dress-making and school teaching. This did not hold back some women taking over a smithy, a pub, a carrier's business, or running a post office or a small shop. In Fringford, for example, after their husbands' deaths, Ann Sirett ran the bakery, Ann Gibbard ran Laurels Farm with her son, and Mrs Ellen Price, followed by Mrs Powell, ran the post office.

The surviving letters of Kezia Whitton and Sarah Butler Rennison tell us something about women's employment. They were both clearly strong and determined Victorian ladies who did not ask for any favours. As we have noted,

Kezia lost four children in infancy, before George and Alexander were born. In 1891, her husband's death left her to run the forge and post office on her own, although she was able to rely to some extent on Freddie Plumb in the forge. She also stayed in close touch with her son, George, and she was even writing him a long chatty letter just five days before she died.[72] Apart from consulting him about a porch, she worries about whether she can fit him and all his family in, as she no longer has a spare bedroom (just like a modern grandmother). She also worries about the number of staff, 'the more people I have about me the more difficult it is to get them to agree..as CKnibbs and Sarah [presumably Sarah Rennison] cant agree no better than Will and Albert could agree in the shop.'

Sarah Butler Rennison (1850-1933) also had more than her fair share of problems to contend with. She met her husband, William Rennison, in London, where she was working as a cook in the 1870s, while he was a valet in the same area. She had a daughter, Nellie (b.1873), but her son, William (b.1874), died aged two. By 1881, Nellie was living with her grandmother, Rhoda, in Fringford. Sarah did not marry William until 1882, shortly before the birth of another son, also called William. By 1891, she was back in Fringford, working as a dressmaker, with William (8), and a lodger, her cousin, Charles Tame (45), who was blind. Her husband seems to have disappeared, and the only subsequent trace of him is in the 1911 census, where he turns up as a visitor in Ireland.

By 1898, the letter from Kezia indicates that Sarah had become a letter-carrier, probably to replace Flora, and it is perhaps no surprise that she is giving Kezia some bother; she would not have stood any nonsense. There were further misfortunes for Sarah, as Nellie's husband, Harry Osborne, became mentally ill and died in 1916. At the same time their daughter, Ivy, died at the age of 19, probably with influenza. All in all, it was not an easy life for Sarah but her letters show her determination. In about 1916, for example, she explains why she does not join the women and children to get crabs [crayfish], 'They can get 1/- per bushel for the government to use the acid in making shells at Birmingham. I don't go as I have to reserve my strength to carry the letters and parcels in the morning.' There is also a very human touch in her letter of 1919, after she had sent an item of jewelry to Florence Butler in Tully, North Queensland, 'I never had much jewellry [sic] in my young days and now I am getting too old; but I have made myself a Black necklace. I wear it when I am dressed up in the summer; and I shall be 70 next April and I shall be a lady at last.'[73] In her last letter of 25 July 1932, when she was clearly not very well and preparing to leave Fringford, she comments 'I want to be quiet and help myself as long as I can. I am leaving no debts. I pay for everything as I have it...I am selling off and giving away. I seem to have collected such a lot.'[74] This is very much in the *Lark Rise* tradition of 'Pay your own way', 'Look after yourself', 'Don't flinch' and avoid 'the House [Workhouse] and dependence on parish relief. In Nellie's letter of 9 February 1933, after Sarah's death, she has an interesting comment on her mother, 'Last April when she was ill at Fringford and I went down and had the doctor off my own bat she was mad as a hatter because I sent for him. She has been very obstinate and would not do anything they wanted her to do.'[75] As feelings of deference weakened (slowly), both Kezia and Sarah followed 'the mid-Victorians' cult of independence and self-help (epitomised of course in Samuel Smiles's best- selling book of that title in 1859)'.[76] This went hand-in-hand with the desire for a reputation of respectability, as witness Sarah's pleasure at feeling 'a lady at last'.

In spite of the major expansion in female employment during the Great War, notably for the Canaries, so-called because their skins turned yellow working in the munition factories, the pre-war attitude to the employment of married women continued in the 1920s. There was little improvement for them and the General Strike of 1926 and the Depression in the 1930s only made men all the more determined to keep their old jobs. Many trades and professions were actively antagonistic, not just to the married woman worker, but also to the idea of all female labour. In the teaching profession, the great majority of local authorities still made difficulties about marriage for female teachers. 'Of the 900,000 married women who go out to work, 300,000 pretend to be single, because often the truth would lose them their jobs.' There was even an association, Fairfield, formed to try to ban the entry of *all* women into the Civil Service [as being] to the detriment of men workers.[77]

As a result, the main changes in women's employment only came well after the Second World War, with increasing numbers entering the professions and working away from home, for example in the City of London. In the village today, it is impossible to tell whether the husband or wife/partner or both are going out to work. In many cases, one or both of them may be working from home, given the opportunities provided by the internet. During the working week, this means that the village can seem as deserted as it did to Flora when she arrived in 1891.

Village shops

By the 1850s, most village shops were trading as grocers and general shopkeepers. In 1851, Amelia Harris, widow, age 43, is listed as a grocer, and George Mansfield, age 47, as carrier, shopkeeper and carriage manufacturer. This illustrates how men were often able to 'multi-task' in Victorian times, but his wife would have run the shop while he combined the carrier's job with building carriages. By 1861, he was listed as a 'proprietor of houses', and his son, John, had taken over the carrier's business. After George's death in 1866, he and his wife must have also taken over the shop in Mansfield Yard, as John was listed as a butcher and grocer in 1871. After his death in 1886, his widow, Mary, continued as a grocer, at least until 1911 when she was 83; she died in 1914. She is described by Flora Thompson as "what was called there 'a little pennicking bit of a woman', small and fair. She was a generous open-handed creature who gave liberally to every good cause. The poor had cause to bless her, for their credit there in bad times was unlimited, and many families had a standing debt on her books that both debtor and creditor knew could never be paid." This sheds light on how close-knit the village community was at the time. Flora refers

Mary Mansfield with her son, Frederick and niece, Mary, outside their grocery store, Church End, early 1890s. (Peter Morrall)

to the grocer's shop as Tarman's, run by 'a burly giant in a very white apron.' She also comments 'This family was not liked by all; some said they had ideas above their station in life, chiefly because the children were sent to boarding-school; but practically everyone dealt at their shop, for not only was it the only grocery establishment of any size in the place, but the goods sold there could be relied upon.'[78]

As we have seen, it was their son, Frederick, who went to Courteenhall Grammar School with the Whitton boys. Their daughter, Matilda, married firstly John Price, who worked with his father as a painter/glaizer [sic]. This must have seemed like the perfect village marriage between two very successful family businesses. Sadly, John died in 1887, and Matilda was a shopkeeper on her own from then until 1895, when she married secondly Ebenezer Sirett. They lived on Rectory Lane. He had been a baker at the Old Bake House with his mother until William Biggers took over in 1901. After that he was listed as a general labourer. The Price ledgers (see Chapter 8) show that he worked part-time in their business and he is often referred to as Ebb. By local accounts, he never worked too hard and may have relied on his wife's money. She died in 1911 but he lived on until 1946.

In 1861, James Gould was listed as a grocer and in 1869 Amelia Harris was still a grocer and Miss Emma Greenwood a shopkeeper, as were Harriet Greenland and Francis Harry Price. Frederick C. Grantham was listed as one in 1903 and 1907. Albert

Carey was listed as a shopkeeper in 1911 but died that year, aged 40, and was succeeded by his wife, Elizabeth (41), who was still running a grocery shop on Rectory Lane in 1939. In the 1920s and 1930s, Miss Ellen Hitchcock and Mrs Emily 'Granny' Wright both had small shops on Rectory Lane and Miss Elizabeth 'Lizzie' Grantham one in Stone Gap Cottage on Main Street.

In the early 1950s, memories of the Second World War were still fresh in people's minds. The period of austerity continued, with rationing for food, clothing, petrol and many domestic products surviving until 1954. In 1941, the weekly meat ration had been as little as half a pound per person, about a shilling's worth (5p), which in a comfortable pre-war household would have constituted a single helping. Weekly rations of other basic foods were similarly meagre: 1oz cheese, 4oz bacon or ham, 8oz sugar, 8oz fats (including not more than 2oz butter) and 2oz jam or marmalade. There were some extra rations for agricultural workers and miners. It may have been a period of austerity but it was not all gloom, as some historians would have you believe. Many people remembered hard times in the 1920s and 1930s and were used to 'getting by' and there was great relief at the arrival of peace. For children, there was also great excitement when it was possible to buy your first bar of chocolate and first ice-cream. Other treats were the first bananas and fresh eggs after all the powdered egg, although, in a rural community like Fringford, fresh eggs and produce from the farms and allotments had been available.

After the War, you could still buy sweets, tobacco and cigarettes from Lizzie Grantham on Main Street or 'Granny Wright' in Prentice's Yard. Miss Hutton, and then the Savins, continued to run 'Mrs Carey's' grocery shop, after her death in the late 1930s. If you called into Mansfield Yard, you could get some supplies from Emily Hinks' shop and pick up your watch from William Elderfield or simply enjoy the wonderful array of clocks and watches in his workshop. You could pick up some milk from Frank Sumner at Church Farm, although he was still delivering daily, carrying two milk churns on a yoke across his shoulders. His dairy was on the site of the present Dairy Cottage, next to Mansfield Yard. You could still buy your bread at the Old Bake House until Les Morgan retired in the late 1960s, and your weekly meat ration from Cecil Cross at Rosecroft.

After all these shops had closed, you could have done at least some of your grocery shopping at Mrs Omar's, a shop at Sunnyside by the cricket ground; it was the last shop to close in the late 1970s. By then, most people were using the regular bus services to Bicester, Buckingham and Oxford to do their shopping. This was a major factor in the decline in the number of village shops but there had also been an increasing number of stores making deliveries, even in the early 1900s. The same might be said today, when you can have your weekly groceries delivered by Tesco, your car washed and even your wheelie-bins cleaned at home.

Post Offices

In 1847, prior to the opening of a sub-post office, the Post Office trade directory records 'Letters received by Thomas Pratt, with horse and cart from Bicester every morning, bringing the Shelswell letter bag; & returns in the evening taking letters for post, charge 1d.' This system must have been mainly for the benefit of the squire at Shelswell Park. By 1883, the Whittons at the Forge had taken on the new Sub-Post Office, Money Order Office & Savings Bank. As we have seen, Flora, Sarah Butler Rennison and Zilpha Hinks were all letter-carriers for them. We have also seen some of Kezia's comments on the bureaucracy of the Post Office, and her fears about possible changes.

After Kezia Whitton's death in 1898, John and Mary Wyatt, who were recently married and living on Rectory Lane, took over the Post Office. It seems that Mary Wyatt (née Scrivener) was already working at the Forge, so would have been familiar with the workings of the Post Office and there would have been no need to move it elsewhere. By 1901, William Biggers had taken it over from the Wyatts and moved it to the Old Bake House. By 1910, he had returned to Eynsham, where he was born, to take over the Swan Public house.

At this point, Ernest and Ellen Price at Pringle Cottage took over the Post Office and here it remained until 1953. Ernest continued to work as a plumber until his death in 1945, while Ellen continued to run the Post Office until 1953, with help from her daughter-in-law, Elsie. As previously noted, there is a revealing reference to Ellen in Mr Corfe's handover letter (see Chapter 6), as 'a most intelligent lady – delightful to talk to.' There is also a nice reference to her in one of Sarah Rennison's letters, written about 1916, after she had been given some money by her brother, Thomas, 'The Post Mistress is very good to me. She is the wife of the son of Plumber Price [John Price] and lives in the same house under the chestnut tree. I can trust her not to tell anyone about my good fortune.'[79] Locally, she is also remembered fondly as someone who would talk to anyone.

The Prices divided the cottage so that the Post Office was on the left end. Old photographs show the post-box and later a telephone kiosk by the front gate. In 1953, the Post Office moved to Mrs Laura Powell at No.6, The Manor, where it was thought to be the smallest one in England. 'Down the muddy track', said a child in 1972 pointing a stubby finger towards the farmyard, 'along by the wall and you'll see a gate. Go in there, past the runner beans and the carrots and that's where it is.'[80] It closed in 1986.

Country carriers

In the nineteenth century, or even earlier in some villages, if the local shops did not satisfy your needs, you could get the local carrier to make purchases for you or take a ride with him to one of the local towns. Every market day, he would set off for town in the early morning with his horse and cart, setting off again in the mid-afternoon to be back home in the early evening. Even then his work was not finished, as he still needed to distribute his purchases round the village. It could mean a 17 hour day. Fringford's carrier links with Banbury began in 1829 with Patric [sic] Butler going to The Flying Horse for the Thursday Market Day. In 1847, there is also mention of 'Francis Wath's cart from Hethe by Frinkford to Bicester, tuesday & friday' and 'John Markham's cart for Bicester, some days'. Carriers normally had a regular slot at one of the inns in Banbury and Butler later used the Plough, at least until 1852. By 1861, he was listed as a farmer, with 45 acres, employing one man. George Mansfield went to the Fleur de Lys from 1835-64. As we have seen, in 1851 he was also listed as a shopkeeper and carriage manufacturer, and by 1861, he was described as a 'proprietor of houses'. Both men are fine examples of ambitious Victorians multi-tasking and moving up the social scale.

It was quite common for a carrier's business to be handed from father to son. After George Mansfield's death in 1866, his son, John, took over the carrier's business but by 1871 he was listed as a grocer and butcher. Similarly, James 'Jimmy' Grantham, went to the Old George, from about 1883 until at least 1911. He was followed by his sons, James Henry and William, who continued to use the Old George until the 1920s. They would call at Cottisford, Juniper Hill, Hethe and Stratton Audley on their weekly runs to Banbury (Thursday) and also go to market days at Bicester (Friday), Brackley (Wednesday) and Buckingham (Saturday). It was common for a carrier to have another occupation, like Butler and Mansfield above. In 1876, Jimmy Grantham was listed as a baker and coal dealer. By 1911, he was listed as a farmer and carrier. His sons also operated as coal dealers and William continued after he ceased being a carrier in the 1920s.

Most local people did not regard a ride with the carrier as cheap (only family members travelled free), and it was also slow and rather uncomfortable. In Juniper Hill in the 1880s, 'it was thought quite dashing to ride with Old Jimmy [Grantham], but frightfully extravagant, for the fare was sixpence (2½p) [to Banbury]. Most people preferred to go on foot and keep the sixpence to spend when they got there.'[81] The carrier also acted as shopping agent, so that you could give him your list and he would bring the items back to you on his return. Many considered this worthwhile in view of the wider range of goods available in the towns. Old Jimmy, for example, 'had a standing order to bring her [Dorcas Lane at the Forge] a dozen of those cakes [Banbury ones] every market day.'[82] Some carriers would also bring goods, like shoes, on approval. Payment was often on tick and you paid the carrier what you could afford. Few records of the carriers survive; no doubt they would have kept rough lists but much was simply from memory. Many carriers and shopkeepers tended to be generous to the poorer families and local pressures were such that there would have been few bad debts.

By the 1930s, Bert Bourton and then Albert Taylor, who operated from Stoke Lyne, were only running services to Bicester. Motor omnibuses had now come on the scene and were operating daily services to Bicester, Buckingham and Oxford, and weekly ones to Banbury on Thursday market day. If only today's villagers were so fortunate!

Travel

Railways

The only station in the Shelswell area was Finmere on the Great Central Railway (GCR), the last main line to be built and the first to be closed. The line opened on 15 March 1899 and closed on 3 September 1966, following the proposals of Dr Beeching in 1962. Soon after the opening, Paxton & Holiday developed a live stock market on land adjacent to the station. The GCR was absorbed by the London & North Eastern Railway in 1923, and, on nationalisation in 1948, the line became part of the London Midland region. Local coal merchants, like Reuben Judd and his sons of Fringford, used to collect coal from the station. During the Second World War, Finmere saw frequent rail movements due to its close proximity to the local airfields and military camps.

Penny Farthings to Porsches

Flora noted another major development in transport 'when the new low safety bicycle superseded the old penny-farthing type.'[83]   The new Raleigh bicycle revolutionised cycling in the 1880s and 1890s, particularly for women. Cycling had been looked upon as a passing craze but in a few years 'there would be at least one bicycle in every one of their houses.'[84] Women's dress was also revolutionised and even if the village women did not wear Amelia Bloomer's new design of women's trousers, they were able to leave most of their petticoats behind in the bedroom.[85] The peak of the craze for cycling came in 1895-7, with 750,000 cycles produced annually. In the early 1900s, photographs of women quite often show them with their new prized bicycle. This allowed them to 'lightly mount "the old bike" and pedal away to the market town to see the shops.'[86] The new bicycles also opened up opportunities for men to travel further for work. In the 1920s, some men locally used to cycle to London for work on a Monday and cycle back on a Friday, while others cycled at least as far as Coventry looking for work.

The next development was the motorcycle, which opened up further possibilities for both men and women from the 1920s. There are many photographs of them with their proud owners in the 1920s and 1930s, often with sidecars. These were ideal for girlfriends or members of the family or to carry your tools for work. It was even possible to attach a mobile smithy to a sidecar. Although cars had been around since the 1890s, only a few could afford them in this period. In Fringford, for example, there were only three cars in the 1930s. Now you can see one, two or more cars outside every house in the village. The cyclists and 'bikers' of the 1920s, to say nothing of Flora, would be amazed to see the occasional gleaming Porsche or Bentley. Apart from all the parked cars, this dependence on the car means that demand for public transport is much reduced and, consequently, there are very limited rural bus services – a real problem for villagers who do not own a car.

Reuben Judd and his sons with their cart in Newton Purcell, probably on their way to collect coal from Finmere Station, early 1900s. (David Judd)

Hunting[87]

Hunting has had a considerable impact on this area for some two hundred and fifty years or more, so this is a story of continuity rather than change. The Bicester Hunt, or the Bicester and Whaddon as it is now known, goes back to 1778. In that time the hunt stables have only been located in three places: Bainton Manor, Swift's House and Stratton Audley. Since the early nineteenth century, a number of trades have been almost entirely dependent on the work provided by the Hunt. For many years these included saddlers, harness-makers, farriers, horse-clippers, breeches-makers, sporting tailors, ostlers and grooms. So much was hand-made that Bicester and Brackley benefited enormously from the Hunt trade. Stratton Audley, as the latest home of the hunting stables, has also benefited since the late nineteenth century. Blacksmiths or farriers have been crucial to them and the Fringford forge also benefited, as we can see in *Lark Rise to Candleford*: 'three times a week, Matthew [Frederick Plumb] and two of the shoeing smiths drove off with strings of horseshoes and boxes of tools to visit the hunting stables.'[88]

Flora gives a colourful description of the annual meet of the Bicester Hunt on the first Saturday in January, which met at the Butchers Arms in Fringford. 'Matthew used to say that it was a funny thing that everybody's errand led them in that direction on Meet Morning.' Matthew himself set a fine example: 'Every year, as soon as the Meet was assembled, Matthew would hang up his apron, slip into his second-best coat, and say that he must just pop across the green for a moment;

Squire, or Sir Austin, or Muster Ramsbottom of Pilvery had asked him to run his hand over his mare's fetlock.'[89] Kezia Whitton also mentions the Hunt in November 1897: 'the other day when the hounds were at Fringford we had a jolly hour or 2 sport- our 3 men and 1 other which was near was called to dig out the Fox just inside diggings at the top of the close for which they all got ½ crown each from Lord Cottenham [Master of the Bicester Hunt 1895-99].' As we have already mentioned, the schoolchildren used to be allowed out to watch the Meet.

Stratton Audley has continued as the centre of the Bicester Hunt to the present day. They still have 49 couples of hounds, receive tremendous support, and in May 2008 new kennels were opened on the original site. In spite of the anti-hunting legislation, the Hunt seems likely to continue to provide enormous pleasure to young and old and employment to many, although they no longer hunt foxes. It must be said that those involved show great respect and understanding of the countryside and country pursuits.

Housing

Rural housing had become a matter of national concern well before the end of the Second World War. In 1943, the government commissioned a survey, for which, out of all England, they chose the Banburyshire region, just to the north of Fringford, for a systematic study and film of rural life under the title 'Twenty-Four Square Miles'. The chosen area included Banbury and was bounded by Hook Norton and the Sibfords in the west, and on the south by Deddington. The film and report highlighted the poor state of rural housing and the extent of the decline in agriculture since the nineteenth century. It revealed that less than one-third of the population was then working on the land. It also showed the dire need for post-war reconstruction. In most of the villages surveyed, electricity and mains water, and new housing, did not arrive until the 1950s or early 1960s. Most families were still using water from wells or the village pumps. After the Second World War, the housing stock in Fringford was in a very dilapidated state. Many of the old cottages, dating from the eighteenth century or earlier, were almost beyond repair and there was little money and few materials available for new building or repairs. At Church Farm House, for example, there are photographs from the early 1960s of a horse eating his dinner in the kitchen and in the lounge! The house was only saved from demolition by new owners. In other cases cottages were simply pulled down and rebuilt or replaced, for example, The Cottage on Crow Lane and a number of cottages on Main Street.

The first improvements in Fringford came in the early 1950s, when they built the council houses in Wise Crescent and on the Stratton Audley Road. These had all the modern conveniences, representing a major advance in the standard of housing in the village. New housing developments followed in Church Close (late 1960s), St Michael's Close (1970s), Manor Road and Crosslands (1980s), and Farriers Close (1990s). In the 1990s, all the council houses in the Stratton Audley Road were further modernised and refaced. In 2012, solar panels were added to them and by then most of them had been sold to their tenants. It should also be said that the improvements in rail travel from Bicester on the Chiltern Line have made Fringford a very desirable, but much more expensive, place to live. There is still the very real threat that the HS2 high-speed line from London to Birmingham will be built; if so, it will pass within two miles of Fringford and might affect house prices.

Friendly Societies

The friendly societies were formed in the nineteenth century to provide some insurance against accident, illness and death for the working classes. Between 1850 and 1875 there was a spectacular increase in the number of these societies, together with that of allied institutions like savings banks. By the end of the nineteenth century, there were some 27,000 registered friendly societies and thousands more that were not registered. In the first half of the nineteenth century, the authorities had been suspicious of such societies, because of their secret passwords and ceremonies. By the 1870s, however, self-help had become an approved form of social progress, and the government had acknowledged the role of the friendly societies and was encouraging membership. This membership came largely from the lower middle down into the lower classes.

The rediscovery of a beautiful silk Oddfellows' banner in the village hall has sparked particular local interest in the friendly societies. A certificate also came to light, hanging unnoticed on a passage wall in the village hall. This was issued on the formation of the Mansfield Lodge of the Independent Order of the Oddfellows (Manchester Unity) on 25th January, 1875. The Mansfield connection was almost certainly with the family who were farming at Hall Farm from the 1850s until the late 1930s.The Oddfellows Friendly Society has a lengthy history, possibly dating back to 1452. However, in modern times, the key date was the formation of the Manchester Unity Order of Odd Fellows in 1813. By 1850, this Order had become the largest and richest friendly society in Britain. By 1911, when Asquith's Liberal Government passed the National Insurance Act, the Oddfellows protected so many people that the government used their actuarial tables to work out the level of contribution and payment required. At this time the Oddfellows was the largest friendly society in the world.

The Fringford banner is of particular interest, as it was made by George Tutill (1817-87) from Howden in the East Riding of Yorkshire. He set up business there in 1837 but by 1857 he had established himself in East London, where there was a large colony of silk-weavers. Over the years, his business was to manufacture more trade union banners than any other in the world, but it was not confined to trade unions. He also made banners and regalia for the Comical Fellows, Free Gardeners, Masons, Bands of Hope, Rechabites, Orange lodges and every kind of friendly society. The regalia included sashes, emblems, aprons, collars and even robes and false beards for the United Ancient Order of Druids![90]

The Oddfellows' Procession with their banner, leaving the church on Feast Day, on its way to enjoy the entertainment on the Green, early 1900s. (Bill Plumb)

A special feature of his work was to have a different painting and inscription on the reverse of the banner, as we found on our banner, with 'All Men Are Brethren' inscribed on one side and 'United We Stand Divided We Fall' on the other. The colours of the banner are still sparkling, as it is has been kept in the original Tutill box. We were also fortunate to have an old photograph from about 1900-10, showing the banner in procession outside Fringford church. Most banners were put away after the defeat of Labour in the Great Strike of 1926, and discussion with some of the older residents seems to indicate that this banner was not carried in procession much after 1920.[91]

It is impossible to know exactly when the Mansfield Lodge purchased the Tutill banner. For a small branch it would have been a major commitment and a major aspiration, costing about £55 in 1890. In the late 1880s, there was 'an orgy of banner-making', reaching a climax in 1889 with the great dockers' strike. Tutills were besieged, for with a Tutill banner, 'a branch *arrived*.'[92] So it is likely that the Mansfield Lodge made the commitment about this time. It was then too that Flora's father, Albert Timms, was a member of the Brackley Rock of Hope Branch of the Oddfellows, which had a monthly club night where he found the talk stimulating. He paid 2s 6d (12.5p) per month and claimed sick pay on a number of occasions.[93]

Flora commented that 'other, more conventional fraternities used at that time to say that the Oddfellows were no better than a lot of old freemasons and this idea was not discouraged by the Oddfellows themselves.' They liked to think of

Club Committee in the 1920s. Front row from left to right: Harry Batchelor, Mark Hutton, Happy Hinks, Bert White, unknown, Bill Wright. Back row: Bill Golder, Twink Hutton, Ernie Watts (Waterloo Farm), 2 unknowns, Arthur Cawston, George Mansfield. (Gordon Allen)

themselves as a secret society and most of the brethren were Liberals with a Radical tinge; 'altogether the Oddfellows were regarded as a daring lot; though, strange as it may appear to some people, their lives were generally exemplary.'[94] Although Fringford was a very conservative and controlled village, I doubt whether the squire or the rector were too troubled by the formation of an Oddfellows lodge. By the 1870s, the Oddfellows and other friendly societies would have seemed quite respectable, and even been encouraged.

The minutes of the Mansfield Lodge from 1933 to 1966 have also come to light in the Oxfordshire History Centre. They show that members of the committee regularly attended the District AGM in Banbury or Buckingham. Sadly, they do not give any indication of the number of members, although a decrease in membership is noted as early as 1935. Neighbouring Tingewick had some 300 members and the Mansfield Lodge may well have had a similar number. There is evidence that membership was not confined to Fringford. Hardwick, Hethe, Juniper Hill and Stratton Audley all seem to have been involved, while Stoke Lyne had their own friendly society by the early 1900s. In 1949, the Mansfield Lodge moved its headquarters from Fringford (probably in the Old Rectory barn) to the old Hethe village hall, opposite the church. There are no minutes from 31 October 1956 to 21 April 1964, when the committee finally agreed to amalgamate with the Loyal Cherwell Valley Lodge, based in Deddington. On 5 April 1966, the Lodge closed, with 'the finances in very good position.' The Cherwell Valley Lodge later merged with a Banbury lodge.

May Queen, Jean Faulkner, with the Revd John Westlake and Len Standen in the back row, early 1950s. (Judy Legg)

The surviving minutes of the Lodge do not provide any details of the membership or their contributions and benefits. However, the neighbouring Grenville Lodge of the Oddfellows in Buckingham, which was formed in 1842, has records going back to 1857. These records provide details of contributions and benefits and the occupations of the members. Although the Grenville Lodge was much larger, it was also a member of the Banbury District, and its records are therefore an invaluable guide to the operations of the Mansfield Lodge. In 1880 the Lodge had some 80 members but by 1911 this had increased to about 800. In these early years, sickness benefit for the first 52 weeks was 12s (60p) and 6s (30p) thereafter, and funeral benefit £20. After the National Insurance Act of 1911, a new scale of contributions and benefits was set. In 1919, further new tables were introduced, which included an annuity after the age of 70. By 1940, there is evidence that most new members were joining from a Juvenile Lodge, aged 16, no doubt many of them the sons of members. The last member, number 1469, was admitted on 5 December 1974.

The listings of the male occupations support the earlier statement that membership of the friendly societies came largely from the lower middle down into the lower classes. Shoemaker, baker, coalman, painter, groom, carpenter, tailor, blacksmith and hurdle maker are just a few of the occupations listed. It is interesting to observe that, at least up to 1914, changes in individual occupations are noted. For example, tailor to collector of taxes, baker to farmer, servant to poultry farmer, shop assistant to cycle agent, labourers to police constable and electrician, and many to jobs on the railway. These reflect men moving with the times and seeking to improve their prospects.

Buckingham also catered for female members of the Oddfellows, by forming the Florence Nightingale Lodge of the Oddfellows (Manchester Unity) in 1898. By 1919 there were 49 members, of whom most of were listed as housewife, with a few as domestic, cook, cashier, shop assistant, laundress or hairdresser. By 1968, there were only seven, and recently there was only one, who had joined at birth.

There was a natural decline in membership of all the friendly societies after the introduction of the National Health Service in 1948. However, there are still some 350 members in the Bedfordshire and Buckinghamshire lodges. The three remaining lodges in Banbury have merged with the Heart of England Lodge in Leamington, and the Chipping Norton branch has merged with North Gloucestershire. In the current period of 'austerity', we might wish to see the return of more self-help and the support which the Oddfellows and other friendly societies used to provide for so many men and women.

Chapter 7 footnotes

57 *Lark Rise*, 417.
58 *Lark Rise*, 246.
59 Pamela Horn, The *Real Lark Rise to Candleford, Life in the Victorian Countryside*, 10 (Amberley, 2012).
60 For this section I am indebted to Joan Goodin, Grace Rutherford, Rhonda Smith and Pat Spence.
61 *Lark Rise*, 39-40. Emma Timms (née Dibber) worked as a nursemaid for the rector of Ardley from 1870 until she got married in 1875 and moved to Juniper.
62 It was Joseph's great granddaughter, Elizabeth Bagley, who sent me copies of Sarah Butler Rennison's letters and her photograph in the back garden of Church Farm House, Fringford. The letters were addressed to her brother, Thomas, and other family members in Australia.
63 Most of the information about 'Fringford' and the brothers, Thomas and Joseph Butler, was provided by Grace Rutherford in her letter and enclosures sent to the author on 9 March 2006.
64 *Lark Rise*, 289.
65 Pamela Horn, *The Rise and Fall of the Victorian Servant*, 36 (Alan Sutton, 1990).
66 Paul Thompson, *The Edwardians: The Remaking of British Society*, 95 (Routledge, 1992).
67 *Lark Rise*, 246.
68 *Lark Rise*, 529.
69 *Lark Rise*, 24-5.
70 G.E.Mingay, *Rural Life in Victorian England*, 191 (Alan Sutton, 1990).
71 J.F.C.Harrison, *Late Victorian Britain, 1875-1901*, 167-8 (Fontana, 1990).
72 Letter from Kezia Whitton to her son, George, 6 February 1898.
73 Letter from Sarah Butler Rennison to Florence Rhoda Butler, daughter of her brother,Thomas Butler, 1919.
74 Letter from Sarah Rennison to her Brother and Sister and Family [probably Thomas Butler and his family], 25 July 1932.
75 Letter from Nellie Dean to Uncle Tom [Butler] and Family, 9 February 1933.
76 Geoffrey Best, *Mid-Victorian Britain 1851-75*, 281 (Fontana 1971).
77 Anne de Courcy, *1939 The Last Season*, 16-17 (Phoenix, 2003).
78 *Lark Rise*, 462-3.

[79] Letter from Sarah Butler Rennison to her brother, Thomas Butler, c.1916.

[80] *Oxford Times*, 8 September 1972.

[81] *Lark Rise*, 254.

[82] *Lark Rise*, 397.

[83] *Lark Rise*, 476.

[84] *Lark Rise*, 255.

[85] *Lark Rise*, 477.

[86] *Lark Rise*, 255.

[87] For a fuller story, see M.W.Greenwood, *In Flora's Footsteps*, 51-63.

[88] *Lark Rise,* 370.

[89] *Lark Rise,* 420.

[90] John Gorman, *Banner Bright, An illustrated history of the banners of the British trade union movement*, 52.

[91] Gorman, *Banner Bright*, 6-19.

[92] Gorman, *Banner Bright*, 7.

[93] Christine Bloxham, *The World of Flora Thompson Revisited*, 134.

[94] Flora Thompson, *Still Glides the Stream*, 159-60 (OUP, 1948).

Chapter 8

The Price Family, 1852-1953

By a stroke of good fortune in the 1990s, the owners of Pringle Cottage in Rectory Lane, passed me some old ledgers which they had found in the rafters. These proved to be some of the business records of the Price family. John Price, with his wife Eleanor, seems to have moved to the village in 1852, to be the publican at the Butchers Arms. By 1863, at the latest, they had moved to Pringle Cottage, where the family lived until 1953. The Prices were plumbers, painters, and glaziers, and the ledgers are some of their business records from 1869 to 1917. In spite of numerous enquiries, I have failed to find any similar records of such a small local business in Oxfordshire. The Price story has been further illuminated by contacts with current members of the family and copies of some of their old photographs. It all helps to shed further light on village life at the time.

The main part of Pringle Cottage was probably built in the eighteenth century. There used to be a barn at the south end and a workshop for the Prices at the north end. By 1852, John Price, who was born in Burford in 1828, was the victualler at the Butchers Arms and also a plumber, painter, glazier and paper hanger. In 1830, he had married Eleanor, who was born at Shotteswell, Warwickshire. It is unclear how

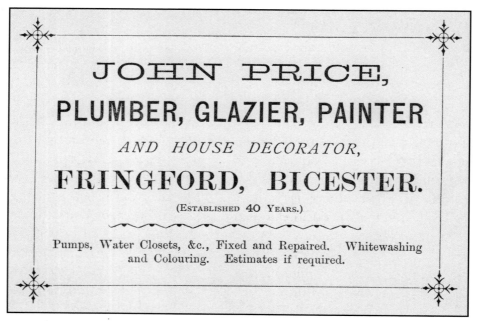

JOHN PRICE,

PLUMBER, GLAZIER, PAINTER

AND HOUSE DECORATOR,

FRINGFORD, BICESTER.

(Established 40 Years.)

Pumps, Water Closets, &c., Fixed and Repaired. Whitewashing and Colouring. Estimates if required.

John Price's business card showing him 'Established 40 Years', 1890s. (Price family)

Pringle Cottage, Rectory Lane. The barn, on left, was later demolished, early 1900s.
(Price family)

long they were at the Butchers Arms but James Hodgkins had taken over by 1863 and he ran the pub until his death in 1890. By 1863, therefore, the Prices were living at Pringle Cottage and John was concentrating solely on his business as a plumber, painter, and glazier (see his business card above). He continued to run the business until his death in 1897, helped by his sons, John (b.1853), William (b.1856) and Francis (b.1861), and later by Ernest (b.1870).

In the late 1870s, as noted above, John married Matilda Mansfield, daughter of George Mansfield, owner of the grocery and butcher's shop. This united two of the most successful families in the village and it must have been the wedding of the year, but sadly John died in 1887. William, who married Alice Spacey, had moved by 1881 to Swanbourne, near Winslow, Buckinghamshire. However, he continued to come over and work as a painter for his father, at least until 1889. Shortly after that, he and his wife took over The Boot public house in Swanbourne. He died in 1902 but Alice was still running The Boot in 1911. After John's death in 1897, Eleanor continued to run the business, with the help of Francis and Ernest, until her own death in 1901. After that the business was run as Price Brothers by Francis and Ernest. Ernest married Ellen Norman, who appears in the 1901 Census as a parlour maid, aged 25, working for the Revd R. Douglas Clarke at the Rectory; she was born in Martinhoe, Devon. An old photograph seems to indicate that their wedding reception took place in the grounds of the Rectory, probably about 1903. They had four children: Cecilia Marjorie (b.1904), Edward Norman 'Eddie' (b.1905), Richard William (b.1907), and Thomas Henry (b.1909). Francis Price had married in the 1880s

TABLE 4

John Price's Customers 1869-77

				Receipts
The Great Houses (3)				**£**
Shelswell Park (Slater-Harrison)				578
Tusmore Park (Earl of Effingham)				630
Stratton Audley Park (George Glen)				809
				£2,017
Gentry (4) and Clergy (8)	(Over £10)			
E.Rousby (Cottisford House)				106
W.Dewar (Cotmore House)				72
Miss Russell, Preston Bissett				137
Dr Sweeny, Heath (sic)				20
Rev H.de Salis, Fringford				31
Rev C.Coker, Fringford				43
Rev F.Salter, Heath				20
Rev T.R.Miller, Goddington (sic)				11
Rev C.Harrison, Cottisford				43
Rev H.Palmer, Mixbury				35
Rev J.Meade, Tingewick, then Newton Purcell				15
Rev E.L.Smith, Chetwode				28
				£561
Farmers (76)	(Over £10)			
J.Simonds (sic), Manor Farm, Fringford				43
Ed & Owen Clarke, Fringford, also ref. to Barton				
Hartshorn Farm & Twyford Villa				48
Edwin Clarke, Tingewick Farm House				30
Henry King, Waterloo Farm, Fringford				48
William Waters, Fringford Mill				30
Gibbard, The Laurels, Fringford				10
William Mansfield, Heath Brade, also ref. to				
Fringford Farm (presumably Hall Farm)				25
Edward Paxton, Willaston Farm				16
H.L.Paxton, Mixbury Middle Farm				56
Edward Harper, Mixbury Lodge Farm				23
Joseph Waters, Cold Harbour, Cottisford				33
William Lambourne, Bainton				53
William Crawford, Newton Purcell				24
Thos & George Badham, Newton Grange				10
Lowndes, Barton Grounds Farm				50
Kinch, Charndon Grounds				48
Thos Harper, Poundon, then Fullwell				20
				£567
Other Customers (41)				**£455**
Total Receipts 1869-77				**£3,600**

and had numerous children but was a widower by 1901. In 1910, Ernest and Ellen took over the village sub-post office from William Biggers at the Old Bake House. No doubt this became Ellen's department, while John concentrated on the family business. The Domesday Valuation of 1910 records 'E.Price, house, shop, P.O., outbuildings & gdn'. It also records Price & others as tenants of Edward Slater-Harrison with 'Closes, some 7 acres, including 2 small pastures and a shed'. There is also a separate record of Price Bros with land of just over an acre, which would have provided space for their horse or horses. It is time now to examine the ledgers in detail and see what they might add to our knowledge of village life.

Ernest Price, c.1903. (Price family)

The Ledgers

The following ledgers, day books and diaries survive:
1. 1869-77 Customer Ledger.
2. 1883-96 Day Book.
3. 1884-96 Cash/Day Book.
4. 1907 Diary.
5. 1916 Diary.
6. 1917 Diary.

Before examining the ledgers in detail, it is worth looking back at some of the changes in village life at the time, as discussed in the previous chapter. John Price will have benefited from the period of high farming in the 1860s, when he was expanding his business after leaving the Butchers Arms. By 1871, Fringford's population was at its peak and enjoying its highest number of tradesmen (41) (see Tables 1 & 3). As we see in the customer ledger of 1869-77, John was now able to introduce his two oldest sons, John and William, into the business, followed later by Francis (Frank) and Ernest. He had plenty of business with the local farmers, who had to weather the agricultural depressions of 1874-84 and 1891-97. His Xmas [sic] billings in the 1890s seem to show that his business held up well. When we come to the diaries for 1916 and 1917, it is well to remember that these were some of the worst years in the Great War, with conscription and food shortages.

1. 1869-77 Customer Ledger

This ledger includes the work done and billed for each customer in the nine years from 1869 to 1877. It is not always easy to determine exactly how much was billed or when it was paid. I have therefore made a best estimate of how much was billed

Price Family: Ellen, Marjorie, Richard, Edward, and Henry on right with unknown lady, Pringle Cottage/Post Office, c.1912. (Price family)

for all the customers in total for this nine-year period. In the summary (Table 4), I have separated the customers into the following categories: Great Houses, Gentry and Clergy, Farmers and Other. It should be noted that sixteen of the Other Customers paid only £34 between them. The total billed comes to some £3,600, which would mean average annual receipts of some £400. This amount is given some credence when we examine the Cash Day Book for 1884-96 below.

The ledger also includes time records and daily charge-out rates for those who worked on some of the larger customers. The work was largely done by Self (John), Frank (FK), John's sons, John and William, Geo (possibly George Mansfield), Ebenezer Sirett (Ebb), and Prosser. Various individual and group daily rates are shown but the following represent a fair sample of rates for a normal 8-hour day: Self (John) 5/3 (26.25p), William 4/3 (21.25p), Self and William 10/0 (50p), Son John and Sirett, Self and Frank or John and Frank 8/0 (40p), Self and Prosser 9/9 (48.75p), and Self, George, William and Frank 16/0 (80p). Frank, who was only aged 15 in 1876, was charged at 2/6 (12.5p). The rates were adjusted for shorter or longer days. It is interesting to consider how much profit the business might have been making on these rates. As the Day Books confirm, a normal week's work was 6 days; Saturday half-days were rare before 1914. So a full six-day week's work for Sirett, for example, at 4/0 (20p) a day, would have earned the business £1.4.0 (£1.20). It is clear that Sirett was not consistently chargeable to customers for a full week. If we assume that he was chargeable on average for four days a week, the business would have earned 16s (80p). It is impossible to say how much Price would have paid Sirett

Pringle Cottage/Post Office, with telephone box, 1930s. (Price family)

but a general labourer at this date would not have expected to receive more than 10s (50p) a week. If Price only paid Sirett for the days he worked, he might only have received some 7-8s (35-40p) against the 16s (80p) recovered from customers. On this basis, Price would have been making a very reasonable profit on his workforce.

2. 1883-96 Day Book

This is a daily record of who was working where and what they were doing. They worked a 6-day week and they were clearly extremely busy. The last few back pages record the costs of some of the work done, mainly in the 1890s, but sadly they do not include any daily rates. It is interesting that the record finishes the year before John Price died in 1897. The ledgers and day books are all well written and it seems likely that it was Eleanor Price who wrote them up for her husband. She died in 1901 and no later customer ledgers have survived.

3. 1884-96 Cash/Day Book

The opening section of this book records the rent collections made for the Lady Day, Michaelmas and Christmas Quarters, 1884-88 and 1896-97. Price collected the rents for a number of cottages in Fringford and Hethe, which were owned by the Shelswell estate (Slater-Harrison). In Fringford in 1884, Ambrose Golder (labourer), Mrs Harris (shopkeeper), and Thomas Wootton were all paying 17/6 a quarter (87.5p), Mr & Mrs Freeman (shopkeeper) 16/0 (80p) for 2 months, while Mr & Mrs John Carey (shopkeeper) were paying £1.6.0 (£1.30) for house and hovel. In Heath [sic], William Claydon was paying 16/6 (82.5p), Mary Jarvis 13/6 (67.5p) and William House £2.5.0 (£2.25) for larger premises.

The book also records related payments for work done on the cottages, quarterly income tax and rates, and commission payable to John Price, which amounted to 11/7 (58p) per quarter. There are also Day Book records for 1889, which show most if not all of the earlier customers. The work force included Self (John), FK (Frank), Ernest (Ern), and Busby, Gibbard, Parker and George on occasion. As we have seen, William (Bill) also continued to work on the team regularly, at least until 1889. There are also lists of Bills for Xmas [sic] for 1893-96, and some miscellaneous work done in the 1890s. The only daily rate recorded is 3/6 (17.5p) for Frank in 1892, an increase from the original 2/6 (12.5p) in 1876.

Ellen Price, Pringle Cottage/Post Office, 1940s. (Price family)

The Bills for Xmas for 1993-96, for some 35 customers, total £148, £141, £176 and £162. These bills total £627, of which £388 is accounted for by just eight customers. Of these, the Earl of Effingham and the Tusmore estate account for £133. Bills were normally sent three times a year, on Lady Day (25 March), Michaelmas (29 September) and Christmas (25 December). If we multiply these figures by three, we get the following rough estimates for annual bills: £444, £420, £528 and £486. These figures suggest that the estimate of £ £400 per annum in the 1870s is reasonable, allowing for some inflation and growth in the business by the 1890s.

4. 1907 Diary
There are only two pages completed at the back of this diary. They relate to work done (£55) and an estimate for repairs (£122) to Fringford Rectory and Glebe Farm for the Revd R. Douglas Clarke.

5. 1916 Diary
This diary is essentially a daily record of who is doing what and where they are working, with very few figures given. The record is of particular interest for the

Tusmore Park, home of the Earl of Effingham, a major customer of the Prices, 1912.
(Wafic Said)

names of customers and the work force. In spite of the war, there are still some 40 customers mentioned, many of them the same as in the 1870s or at least the same properties. There was still significant work for the Shelswell and Tusmore estates, and at Stratton Audley Park for Col and Mrs Gosling, who had succeeded George Glen. Work also continued for a good number of farms and now included Dimmocks Farm, next to Fringford Lodge. Given conscription, there must have been a shortage of young men to work on the farms and elsewhere. The Price work force now included Self (Ernest), FK (Frank), Slatter, Lane, Palmer and Fathers, but no daily rates are given. The last four men do not appear in the 1911 census for Fringford, so they were either newcomers or from one of the neighbouring villages. Slatter is a Fringford name, while Lane and Fathers are Hethe names.

6. 1917 Diary

This is a similar record to the 1916 diary. There seem to be fewer customers but there is a notable amount of time spent at Shelswell, Tusmore and Stratton Audley Park. At one point the team spent 27 days at a stretch, excluding Sundays, working at Shelswell. There was also considerable work for the Chinnerys at Fringford Manor, on the house, gardens and greenhouses. Work for a number of farms continued and now included Pimlico Farm. The work force now included James and Gerring, which are both Fringford names.

Work Done

John Price's business card shows that he thought of himself first and foremost as a plumber, but also as a glazier, painter and house decorator. Much of the work described in the customer ledger for 1869-77 involved pipes, pumps, gutters, boilers, closets, and regular purchases of sheet lead and lead pipe. Work for the local farmers seems to indicate that they were all dairy farmers, as the work included repairs to milk heads, butter churns, cream cisterns, cream bowls and tins, and buckets, pumps and valves, including numerous new ' leathers' i.e. washers. There was also significant work involved in house painting and papering, and glazing and mending windows. In general, if you needed an odd job done, you called the Prices. They even repaired tea pots and toast racks and varnished croquet balls!

It appears that bills were sent regularly, on completion of the work or at the three Quarter Days. Payment also seems to have been reasonably prompt and sometimes involved settlement in kind, for example, with potatoes, old lead, one fat pig (£4.6.0) or 5 pigs (5 @18/6 = £4.2.6).

1917-53

Trade directories indicate that the business ran as Price Bros until Frank Price retired, in or about 1931. At this point the trade directory records Ernest as a plumber on his own and he was still listed in 1939. The brothers both died in 1945, Francis aged 84, Ernest 74. They had certainly enjoyed a long and successful partnership and it is fitting that they are buried side-by-side just inside the gate to Fringford churchyard. After Ernest's death in 1945, Ellen continued to run the post office with the help of Elsie, wife of Eddie. After Eddie and Elsie left the village in 1953, the post office was transferred to Mrs Laura Powell in No.6 The Manor. In the late 1950s, the barn and the workshop at Pringle Cottage were both converted to become part of the main house. The present owners are carrying out further alterations and refurbishment.

Conclusion

The story of the Price family and their business has been richly illuminated by the discovery of these ledgers. They are a rare find and reveal some fascinating information about the extent and nature of a local business in late Victorian times and well into the twentieth century. The family and their staff worked long and hard over a long period and provided an indispensable service to the great houses, the gentry and the clergy, the farmers and numerous smaller customers. It is very difficult to measure the relative value of their income in today's terms. If you simply multiply John Price's estimated income of £400 in the 1870s by the percentage increase in the Retail Price Index (RPI), it gives you a value of £33,000. I am not sure how much this tells you, except that he was making a good living. His income had increased by the 1890s, and the later diaries show that he retained a loyal corps of customers. John, and his sons after him, clearly worked very hard and their success was well-deserved. It is a tribute to John, who started the business in the 1850s that his son, Ernest, was still in business in 1939.

Chapter 9

The Roll of Honour

'When you go home today, tell them of us and say,
For your today, we gave our tomorrow.'[95]

The year 2014 saw worldwide interest in the centenary of the start of the First World War on 4 August 1914. Special services of commemoration were held all over the country on the day and there was a massive build up to Remembrance Day on 9 November. This included Paul Cummins' 'Blood Swept Lands and Seas of Red' display of ceramic poppies at the Tower of London, where 888,246 poppies were planted, one for each British casualty. It really caught the imagination of the public and it was thought that some five million went to see it. After a service there on Armistice Day, the display was dismantled and the poppies dispatched to the thousands who had bought them.

On the local scene, there was a special benefice service at Finmere on 4 August 2014. At the same time, Fringford, largely thanks to Kevin Tobin, raised the money to refurbish the war memorial and re-engrave the names on it. The work is expected to be completed shortly. He has also worked hard to identify all those from the village who fought and returned safely from the Great War. As usual, the service at Fringford on Sunday 9 November 2014 included the Two Minute Silence at the war memorial. Research has shown that the first ceremony held at the new war memorial was at 10.45am on 11 November 1923, after which the people entered the church singing 'O God Our Help in Ages Past'. The names of Fringford men who died in both World Wars are engraved on the war memorial and they are listed below, along with the names of those who have been identified as fighting in the Great War and returning.

1914-18 Names on the War Memorial

Frederick James Batchelor, son of Robert and Anne Batchelor of Green Farm, Fringford. Private 306529, 1st/8th Battalion, Royal Warwickshire Regiment, died 27 August 1917, age 23. Tyne Cot Memorial (Ypres), Panel 23 to 28 and 163A.

John William Gerring, son of James (Jimmy) and Jane Gerring, of Main Street, Fringford. Private 84598, 11th Company, Machine Gun Corps (Infantry), died 22 December 1917, age 23. Windmill British Cemetery, Monchy-le-Preux, Pas de Calais,

Plot 1, Row H, Grave 8. Jimmy Gerring was the sexton for many years and lived in an old cottage on the site of Rosemary Cottage on Main Street. John was a cousin of the Marriotts (see below). In 1911 he was living in Surrey.

Charles Thomas Marriott, Private 201893, 2nd/4th Battalion, Oxfordshire and Buckinghamshire Light Infantry, died 21 March 1918, age 21. Pozieres Memorial, nr. Albert, Panel 50 and 51. Mrs Marriott was a sister of Jimmy Gerring, so Charles Marriott and John Gerring were cousins.

Charles Ernest Richardson, son of the late Charles and Mary Ann Richardson, of Fringford. Private 18398, 11th Battalion, Royal Warwickshire Regiment, died 9 October 1917, age 21. Thiepval Memorial, Pier and Face 9A 9B and 10B. His mother was an assistant teacher at Fringford School from 1871-92

Jack Gerring, killed in action 1917.
(Sue Gahan)

when she got married. She continued to live in Lilac Cottage until her death in 1946, aged 92. Sadly, after losing her son, her daughter, Ada Sophia, died in 1919, aged 25, probably during the great flu epidemic.

Alfred Waring, son of Henry and Jemima Waring, of Fringford, and husband of Mrs A.Waring of Rectory Cottage, Tingewick, Bucks. Private 968, Royal Buckinghamshire Hussars, died 21 August 1915, age 38. Helles Memorial, Gallipoli Peninsula, Turkey, Panel 16 and 17. Alfred was probably older brother of another Henry Waring, who was living at Rose Cottage, Rectory Lane in 1913. His son's wife was the Infants teacher at Fringford School in the 1930s and early 1940s. She moved later to Fringford House on Main Street.

Other Casualties in the Great War
Three other men who died in the Great War are commemorated in the church. Two of them were members of the Revd Cadwallader Coker's family, and their names are recorded on the plaques below the second window in the north aisle, which was dedicated to the Cokers in 1898.

Cadwallader John Coker, younger son of James Gould and Florence Emily Coker, of Mayfield, Sussex: 'Lt, Welsh Regiment, killed in action at St Eloi, 22 June 1915, age 23. Ridge Wood Military Cemetery, Dickebusch, Flanders, Plot 1, Row E.'

Alexander Y. Crawshay Mainwaring Spearman R.N., husband of Jessie Aubrey Loch (formerly Spearman), of Crediton, Devon, daughter of the Revd Cadwallader Coker: 'Commander, Collingwood Battalion, R.N.D. Killed in action in the Dardanelles, 4 June 1915, age 52. Helles Memorial, Gallipoli Peninsula, Turkey, Panel 1 and 2.'

James Dixon is commemorated on a plaque by the south door. He was the brother of Mrs Ellis Chinnery and son of Mr J. Dixon, of Kensington: 'Captain (Adjutant), 2nd Battalion, Middlesex Regiment, fell in action at Neuve Chapelle, 10 March 1915, age 30. Royal Irish Rifles Graveyard, Laventie, Pas de Calais, Plot III, Row K.'

The Boer War 1899-1902

Edward John Dewar is commemorated in the first window in the north aisle. He was a member of the squire's family and died during the Boer War: 'Captain 60th Rifles, died 20 February 1900 of wounds received in action at Paardeburg, South Africa, while serving with the Mounted Infantry, age 36.'

Two village families are known to have been represented in the Boer War. William Grantham was a private in the Prince of Wales's Own, and he received an engraved clock and barometer from the village on his return from the war. In the 1911 Census he was listed as a carrier and farm worker. Fred White also served in the war and received the same gifts from the village; in 1911 he was listed as a horseman and carter on farm. The South African War, as it was generally called at the time, aroused considerable reaction in England, particularly after the Relief of Mafeking, which was defended by Baden-Powell for seven months. The Relief was widely celebrated in most towns and villages and there was a special public holiday on 25 May 1900. The return of the soldiers would have been an emotional moment and these special gifts to William and Fred from the village would have been a natural response.

Fringford Men who fought in the Great War and returned

Charles Frederick Alger (1893-1948), of No.6 Fringford, Queen's Own Oxfordshire Hussars.

Walter George Barnes, born 1895, son of George, shepherd on farm, and Sarah. They may have lived in Mansfield Yard later. Walter was a farm labourer in 1911. 8th Battalion, Oxfordshire and Buckinghamshire Light Infantry.

Henry Bateman, born 1887, son of James, labourer, and Emily, who were living in Hall Farm Cottage in 1891. Royal Engineers, Inland Waterway Transport Unit.

Walter S. Baughan, born 1874, son of Samuel, farm bailiff for the Revd Edward Withington at Fringford Lodge in 1901.Walter was a coachman. Royal Engineers driver.

Arthur Bottrell, born 1873, Dragoon Guards.

William Cadd, born 1865, Royal Horse Artillery.

George Carey, born 1865 in Oddington, son of John Carey and his first wife. Served in the Imperial Yeomanry in South Africa. In First World War, 10th Battalion, London Regiment.

Archie Carey, born 1891, son of John, labourer, and Maria, younger half-brother of George. In 1911 he was living in Northants, married to Edith. No.512, Oxfordshire and Buckinghamshire Light Infantry.

Ellis Haldane Chinnery (1875-1957), son of Henry and Marion of The Manor, Fringford. Queens Own Oxfordshire Hussars.

William Henry Elderfield (1887-1954), married Mary (d.1969), watch and clock repairer. He lived in Mansfield Yard, where he had a separate workshop. He was a blacksmith when he joined the army during the First World War, where his delicate touch was discovered and he was trained as a watch repairer. No trace of his regiment.

William A.Fenemore, born 1898, son of William, miller at Fringford Mill, and Sarah, older brother of Harry and Cyril. He was a houseboy in 1911. No.2882, Queens Own Oxfordshire Hussars.

Harry Fenemore, born 1900, younger brother of William. Royal Navy.

Cyril Fenemore, born 1902, younger brother of Harry. Royal Navy.

Thomas Busby Gerring, born 1893, son of James, a road contractor, and Jane. No.11040, Oxfordshire and Buckinghamshire Light Infantry.

George Arthur Gerring, born 1901, younger brother of Thomas. No.537195, Tank Corps.

Arthur John Golder (1902-59), Tank Corps.

William George Golder, born 1893, son of Ambrose, a carter, and Emma. He was a labourer in 1911. No.14477, 8th Battalion, Oxfordshire and Buckinghamshire Light Infantry.

Albert Edward Green, he ran the Butchers Arms from 1913 to 1955. In 1911 he was married to Ellen Louisa. He died in 1959. His son, Phil Green, lived at 31, Stratton Audley Rd until his death c.2000. T/328885, Army Service Corps, driver.

Hubert Gerald Hancock, born in Northants c.1896. 'Bert', who lived at Green Farm, was baker for Harold Crook at the Old Bake House and ran it from the late 1930s. His son, Gordon John, died in the Second World War (see below). No.146625, Army Service Corps, baker.

John Hing, born 1892, No.7988, Imperial Yeomanry.

Ernest William Hinks (1879-1964), a carpenter and son of Henry and Elizabeth, he married Emily Blencowe, and they had four children, including Gladys, who still lives in St Michael's Close, aged 96. They lived in Mansfield Yard. 491 Field Company, Royal Engineers.

Arthur William Hitchcock, born c.1894. In 1951 he is listed with Evelyn and Fanny E. No.14512, 8th Battalion, Oxfordshire and Buckinghamshire Light Infantry.

Herbert Gladstone Ives, born in Surrey c.1882. His wife, Salome Neal, lived in Church Cottages, aged 18 in 1901, daughter of George (53) and Martha (52). She was a school teacher. No.186962, Imperial Yeomanry.

Edward Jaycock, born 1874. No.3306, 4th Battalion, Oxfordshire and Buckinghamshire Light Infantry.

William James Marriott, in 1911 he was living in Fringford, aged 16, with James and Sarah Gerring. Probably the older brother of Charles Marriott, killed in 1918 (see above). The Gerrings and Marriotts were cousins. Army Service Corps, Forage Department.

Albert Edward Mitchell, born 1899, son of William (45), shepherd on Cotmore farm, and Fanny (38). They had 6 children. In 1911 he was living in Berkshire. No.48542, Royal Berkshire Regiment. Killed but not listed on the Fringford war memorial.

Ernest James Mitchell, born 1896, older brother of Albert, No.203240, Oxfordshire and Buckinghamshire Light Infantry.

Arthur Henry Perry, born 1894 but no record of him living in Fringford up to 1911. No. 192777, Army Service Corps, Motor Transport.

Albert Edward Pollard, born 1885 but no record of him living in Fringford up to 1911. No.82156, Royal Field Artillery.

William James Pratt, no record of him living in Fringford up to 1911. No.39635, Warwickshire Regiment.

Albert Price, born 1891, son of Francis, painter and decorator, and Elizabeth. He was also a painter and decorator but notoriously eccentric and unreliable. No trace of his regiment.

Albert White (1877-1965), a brickmaker, nephew of William and Sarah White. In 1913 he may have been living in Mansfield Yard. He worked at the brickworks on Fringford Hill. No.19602, 5th Battalion, Oxfordshire and Buckinghamshire Light Infantry. His daughter became Dorothy Sparrow. In 1951 Albert and Clara White were living at 4, Council Houses, and in 1958/59 at 4, The Green. They both died in 1965.

George Wright, born 1894, son of William, a groom, and Emily. In 1911 he was living in Northamptonshire. No.18876, 1st Battalion, Oxfordshire and Buckinghamshire Light Infantry.

1939-45 Names on the War Memorial

John Edward Blake (always known as Jack), son of Walter and Anne Blake and husband of Elsie Nellie Blake, of Twyford, Bucks. Private 105892529, R.O.A.C., died 15 March 1945, age 37. Buried at Schoonselhof Cemetery, Antwerp, Plot IV, Row B, Grave 1.

Gordon John Hancock, son of Hubert Gerald and Constance Annie Hancock of Eaton Socon, Bucks. Driver T/5383004, 18 Supply Group, R.A.S.C., died 25 July 1943, a POW, age 23. Kanchanaburi War Cemetery, Thailand (129 km NW of Bangkok), Plot 4, Row A, Grave 50. Locals say that he should never have been signed up, as he was not strong enough.

Leslie Morgan, former village baker at the Old Bake House, also deserves a special mention. He was a Flight Sergeant in 115 Squadron in the RAF, where he served as

Left: John Blake, died March 1945. (Margaret Crawford)
Right: Les Morgan (on right) with an RAF friend, 1940s. (Clive Morgan)

an air gunner and wireless operator. His squadron was equipped with Lancaster bombers and, owing to the type of targets allocated to them, they had the highest casualty rate of any in Bomber Command. His logbook (kept by his son Clive) shows that he flew 38 missions over Germany, including several of the massive bomber raids. In 1947, he was awarded the Belgian Croix de Guerre with Palm. He flew transport missions in India after the German raids. In the village he never spoke of his wartime experiences and he was more famous for the quality of his cakes. He and his wife ran the Stratton Audley Post Office after he gave up the bakery.

Home Guard and Air Raid Precautions (ARP) in the Second World War

Fringford was a high activity zone with airfields at Bicester, Finmere and Upper Heyford. There was also a satellite aerodrome and holding depot on the Shelswell Estate, where everything from Brengun Carriers to Spitfires was hidden in the woods.

George Crowe from Gardeners Cottage was in command of the (LDV) Home Guard at the start of the Second World War. When Bicester was bombed he ordered Fringford villagers to take cover in their homes. Residents who lived near the Manor sometimes went to its cellars as the planes passed over. Harry Wise took over after George Crowe.

The ARP meeting place was a hut by the yew tree at Laurels Farm. The hut was also an Off Licence during the 1940s and early 1950s. Apart from George Crowe, the following were ARP wardens: James Wyatt of Manor Farm, Harry Bachelor, Arthur Brandrick of Cotmore, and some others from the parish. The wardens were called by the siren at Bicester Aerodrome when bombers were on route to Coventry. The duty wardens cycled round the village blowing a whistle and when it was all clear they cycled round ringing a bell. Tanks came to practice manoeuvres at Manor Farm.

In 1940 they smashed down two of James Wyatt's gates and drove over the iron railings surrounding the Manor gardens. There was also a section of the Home Guard based at Hethe, probably with Thomas Allen of the Bike Shop in charge.

There were of course so many others who did not survive these and other wars to lead happy or healthy lives. Perhaps the last moving words should come from Flora Thompson, as she stood in Cottisford church in front of the memorial put up after the Great War and remembered the deaths of her brother, Edwin [Edmund], and other local boys::

'And all the time boys were being born or growing up in the parish, expecting to follow the plough all their lives, or, at most, to do a little mild soldiering or go to work in a town. Gallipoli? Kut? Vimy Ridge? Ypres? What did they know of such places? But they were to know them, and when the time came they did not flinch. Eleven out of that tiny community never came back. A brass plate on the wall of the church, immediately over the old end house seat is engraved with their names. A double column, five names long, then, last and alone, the name of Edmund.'[96]

Chapter 9 footnotes
[95] Attributed to John Maxwell Edmonds (1875-1958).
[96] *Lark Rise,* 247.

Chapter 10

Conclusion

'She was never to see any of these [landmarks] again, but she was to carry
a mental picture of them, to be recalled at will, through the changing
scenes of a lifetime.'[97]

'But I'll remember, and perchance we'll borrow
Long after from the child you put away.'[98]

There must be hundreds of villages in Oxfordshire and elsewhere with a similar
history but the ones in Lark Rise Country are the only ones to have had the good
fortune to be portrayed by Flora Thompson. We should be eternally grateful that
she was able to 'borrow long after from the child she put away'. She had left
Fringford in 1897 and *Lark Rise*, the first part of her trilogy, was not published until
some forty years later in 1939. The discovery of her letter to Miss Eagle does much
to settle the debate about the extent to which the trilogy is autobiographical. As she
explains, *'Lark Rise'* is as far I could make it a faithful portrait of the little Oxfordshire
hamlet where I spent my childhood.' 'In Candleford and Candleford Green I wrote
more freely, intending to give rather a picture of country life at that time and to
portray some of the country characters I had known.' Her stories and characters
leap from the page and make her portrayal of daily life in the late nineteenth century
arguably the greatest book of its kind, and one written by a 'child of poverty'. As we
have seen, even if it is not strictly autobiographical, it tells us so much about daily
life in Fringford at the time.

In the fifteen years since *Fringford Through the Ages* was published, the BBC
Television adaptation of *Lark Rise to Candleford* has introduced a great many people
to the world of Lark Rise Country and made some of the characters, like Queenie
and Twister, household names; it has also brought an influx of new visitors to the
area. A variety of new sources has also emerged, including 'the letters of the three
ladies'. Flora Thompson's letter to Miss Eagle has been a revelation, and the letters
from Kezia Whitton and Sarah Butler Rennison have brought a very human and
personal touch to village life at the time. The Price family's business ledgers, a
remarkable survival, have provided rare details of a successful local business in the
same period. A further bonus has been the research done by Australian descendents
of the Butler family, which brings a very personal slant on emigration to Australia.

The family and their 'Fringford' farm played a significant role in the life of the early pioneers. Their story serves to remind us just how many families today have ancestors who emigrated to Australia and elsewhere in the years 1870 to 1914.

There is still much in the village to interest Flora's admirers and much that she would recognise, in spite of all the changes. The population has doubled since 1951 to over 600 and most of the green spaces have been filled in. The old forge is silent, much farmland is 'set aside' and all the shops are closed. In many families, both parents are now working and commuting away from the village. It is easier for them to do the shopping weekly at the supermarket and much more difficult for any village to support a shop. There may not be the range of craftsmen and tradesmen that there were in Flora's day but the new generation of residents possesses a great variety of skills. There are still some farmers, with teachers, lawyers, surveyors, doctors, nurses, businessmen and women, builders, carpenters, a thatcher, and all manner of computer experts. The village may not be as closely-knit or self-supporting, but the range of activities which the village supports seems to be expanding. The Cricket Club continues to flourish, the School numbers are over the one hundred mark, and the Playgroup thrives. The newly refurbished Village Hall is the venue for a great variety of activities and entertainment, and Candleford Fair is held every summer.

Church attendance may be at an all-time low but each of the ten Shelswell parishes still has its own active church, and there are plans for major refurbishment of Fringford church to make it more welcoming. However, with declining attendance and a shortage of clergy, it is becoming increasingly difficult for the Shelswell Benefice to maintain and service ten churches and for all the parishes to pay their shares to the Diocese. There is a vital need for a new strategy, which might well include closure or mothballing some churches, more services taken by lay people and more of them held in private houses, like the Methodist ones in Lark Rise.

For the future, many of us may wish, like the Hobbit, for 'more green and less noise' but that is impossible. The major developments in Bicester envisage today's population of some 40,000 doubling in the next ten years to more than 80,000, and the green spaces between Fringford and Bicester are likely to be filled one day.

In these difficult and uncertain times, both socially and economically, perhaps we should be looking back to the people of Lark Rise Country, like Kezia Whitton and Sarah Butler Rennison, with their 'don't flinch' and 'self-help' attitude. This included a determination to avoid the workhouse and any dependence on parish/public relief, in modern terms, the benefit system. As feelings of deference weakened (slowly), both Kezia and Sarah followed the mid-Victorians' cult of independence and self-help, which went hand-in-hand with the desire for a reputation of respectability; we have seen Sarah Butler Rennison's pleasure at feeling 'a lady at last'. For all the changes in society since the days of Flora Thompson, let us hope that Fringford will continue to retain its community feeling and separate identity, as it has done for the last two thousand years.

Chapter 10 footnotes

[97] *Lark Rise*, 537.

[98] The last lines from a quotation written out by the author's father; not referenced but almost certainly from Tennyson.

APPENDIX 1

Fringford Tithe Award of 1848, with part of the Tithe Map of 1856
(References are to the 1856 map)

Ref. No.	Landowner (Tenant)	Occupier	Name of property
1	JH Slater-Harrison (JHS-H)	Thos. Simons	Homestead orchard garden
2	do	do	Home close
3	do	do	Dairy ground
4	do	do	garden
5	do	JHS-H	Plantation
6	do	Thos. Simons	Little meadow
7	do	do	Ozier bed meadow
8	do	do	Ozier bed
9	do	do	Newton meadow
10	Eton College (JE Rousby)	GS Waters	Mill holm
11	do	do	Mill leys
12	JHS-H	Thos. Simons	Lower heath
13	do	Himself	Middle heath
14	do	Thos. Simons	Upper heath
15	James Grantham	Himself	Home close
16	Viscount Sidmouth	GS Waters	New close
17	do	John Mansfield	New close
18	Thos. Flowers	Thos. Bailiss	New close
19	JHS-H	Thos. Simons	Diggins
20	do	do	Swains meadow
21	do	do	Pendalls ground
22	do	do	Ashills meadow
23	do	do	Ryehill meadow inc.Freeboard
24	William Mansfield	Himself	Garden
25	George Mansfield	Himself	Garden
26	David Mansfield	Himself	House & garden
27	Wm Mansfield	Himself	House & garden
28	George Mansfield	Himself	House outbuildings & yard
29	JHS-H	Thos. Simons	Beaufoots close
30	John Cotterell	Himself	Garden
31	John Mansfield	Himself	Waters close
32	JHS-H	Thos. Simons	May's close
33	Thos. Flowers	Thos. Bailiss	Smiths close
34	Viscount Sidmouth	John Mansfield	Walnut tree close
35	JHS-H	Thos. Simons	Ladymans close
36	Viscount Sidmouth	John Mansfield	Home close
37	JHS-H	Thos. Simons	Peakes close
38	do	do	Bulls close
39	Viscount Sidmouth	John Mansfield	School House close

Ref. No.	Landowner (Tenant)	Occupier	Name of property
40	JHS-H	Thos. Simons	Barretts close
41	Viscount Sidmouth	John Mansfield	Saul's close
42	Revd HD Roundell	Himself	Gibbs close
43	do	do	Douglas close
44	Eton College (JE Rousby)	GS Waters	Home close
45	do	do	Meadows
46	do	do	Orchard
47	Revd HD Roundell	Thos. Wrighton	Homestead & garden
48	do	do	Close
49	JHS-H	Thos. Simons	Cotts close
50	William Tame	George Mansfield	Wesears close
51	JHS-H	Thos. Simons	Spaceys or Knibbs close
52	William Tame	George Mansfield	Home close
53	JHS-H	Thos Simons	Home close
54	do	do	Twenty lands
55	Thos. Flowers	Thos. Bailiss	Home close
56	Eton College (JE Rousby)	GS Waters	Twenty lands
57	JHS-H	Thos. Simons	Pit piece
58	do	do	Upper Mangton or the Butts
59	do	do	Lower Mangton
60	do	do	Crabtree Piece
61	do	do	do
62	Thos. Flowers	Thos. Bailiss	Part pf Pinhill close
63	JHS-H	John King	Pinhill close
64	Viscount Sidmouth	John Mansfield	Hedgeway
65	JHS-H	John King	Colehill meadow
66	do	do	Colehill
67	do	do	Middle ground
68	do	do	Hedgeway
69	Viscount Sidmouth	John Mansfield	Waddington's close
70	JHS-H	John King	do
71	do	do	Lords mead
72	do	do	Stretchill ground
73	Viscount Sidmouth	John Mansfield	Beggars bridge
74	JHS-H	John King	Barn ground
75	do	do	Stone pit ground
76	do	do	Bainton ground
77	do	do	Home close
78	do	do	Homestead, garden & orchard
79	do	do	First furze ground
80	do	do	Meadow
81	do	Himself	Cotmoor Wood
82	do	do	Lower furze
83	do	do	Upper furze

Notes:

1. Under the Tithe Award, tithes (a tenth part of a person's income paid to the rector in cash or kind) were commuted to a rent-charge.
2. J.H.Slater-Harrison (JHS-H) owned 50 of the properties, of which Thomas Simons occupied 30.
3. Parcels 10, 11, 44, 45, 46, and 56 were the property of Eton College, whose leaseholder was James Edward Rousby. The occupier of all the parcels was George Stimson Waters, who was a farmer, brewer, maltster and miller with 100 acres and 6 labourers at the time.
4. Parcels 10 and 11 covered Fringford Mill and parcels 44-46 Church Farm.
5. Parcels 56-73 covered the fields on either side of the Caversfield Road down to the crossroads.
6. Parcels 74-83 covered Cotmore, Moat Farm and the area beyond the crossroads.

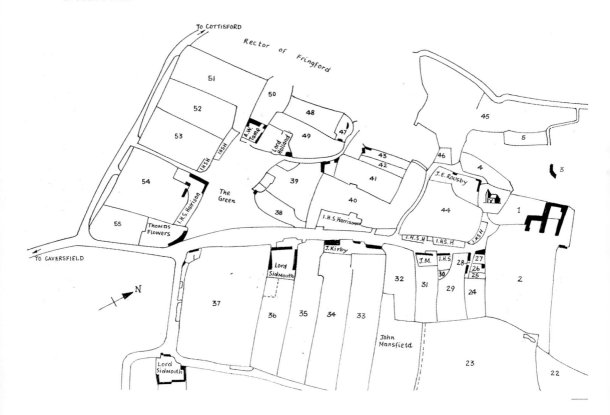

Tithe Map of 1856

APPENDIX 2

Lloyd George "Domesday" Valuation, 1910

The 1909-1910 Finance Act provided for the levy and collection of a duty on the increment value of all land in the United Kingdom. The Board of Inland Revenue were required to ascertain the site value of all land in the UK as on 30 April 1910. Two sets of books were created: the Valuation or so-called Domesday Books and the Field Books (1912-15). The property description in the Field Books is more detailed than in the Valuation Books. A Form 37 (1912-15), based on the information in the Field Books, was also completed for each property, and a copy was given to the owner of the property. Lloyd George was the master-mind behind the Valuation, hence it is commonly referred to as the Lloyd George Domesday Valuation. The value ascertained formed the base valuation or datum for calculating the Increment Value Duty

These records provide some fascinating information about the properties and inhabitants of the village in this period, although it must be said that it is not the easiest source for any local historian. This is because the records are split between the Oxford History Centre (OHC) and the National Archives at Kew, which keeps the Field Books (see Bibliography). The information usually includes the names of the owner and occupier and the area covered by the property; also the number of rooms and the state of repair. Valuation figures normally include the market value of the fee simple of the whole property and the market value of the site divested of structures, timber and plants. The assessments of site value continued until the Increment Value Duty was repealed by the Finance Act of 1920.

APPENDIX 3

Courteenhall Free Grammar School, Northampton

The School

Courteenhall Free Grammar School, a few miles south of Northampton, was founded by Sir Samuel Jones and erected in 1680. He endowed it with £100 yearly and £20 for apprentices. The main house and stables, in a park of some 90 acres, were built c.1770 for the Wake family by John Carr of York. They were built on a very grand scale, possibly to compete with neighbouring Althorp. The Wakes moved here when their main house at Waltham Abbey was burnt down, and the family still live here. In 1885, average attendance was 30, all the boys were taught free and there was an adjoining house for the master. There was also an Infants School, attended by 20 children, supported by voluntary contributions. The school closed in 1898 but reopened in 1923 as a Church of England (Infants) Elementary School. It closed c.1945/46. The Old School Room survives with the original oak seats and the tall masters' desks and it is still used for parish meetings.

The School Register

The School Register, 1854-90, can be seen at the Northamptonshire Record Office (Box V665). The following is a sample of the curriculum from the Register in the 1870s, when George and Alexander Whitton and Frederick Mansfield attended the school. It is interesting that their studies included some science subjects:

Monday	Wednesday	Thursday
Script	Script	Script
Lat Gram	Lat Gram	Latin Gram
Delectus (see note)	Exercise	Exercise
Chemistry	Delectus	Delectus
Writing	Mechanics	Chemistry
Dictation	Writing	Writing
Math	Dictation	Dictation
History	Math	Math
Divinity	Geography	History
	Divinity	Divinity

Note: Delectus = school reading book of selected passages (OED)

APPENDIX 4
Fringford Rectors 1100-2014

1103	Earliest evidence of a church at Fringford. No evidence of a rector.
c.1215	Robert Pilcher
1233	Robert Lovel
1480-1523	Thomas Kirby
1565-1604	Richard Aldrich
1604-34	Emmanuel Scott
1634-45	William Overton (deposed)
1645-48	John Bayley (deposed by Cromwell)
1660-97	John Bayley (returned under Charles II)
1697	Matthew Fantoux (died same year)
1697-1726	Bernard Gilpin
1726-41	Joseph Barnes
1735-56	Daniel Wardle, Curate in charge 1741-53, Rector 1753-56.
1756-1813	John Russell Greenhill
1814-52	Henry D. Roundell
1852-73	Henry J. de Salis
1873-94	Cadwallader Coker
1894-98	Charles S. Thompson
1898-1910	R. Douglas Clarke
1910-21	Stafford Meredith Brown
1921-24	Archdeacon Whylock Pendavis, Rector of Fringford & Hethe from 1924.
1925-31	Leslie Brasnett
1931-48	John Harrington
1948-53	Horace Jones
1954-63	John Westlake, Rector of Newton Purcell with Fringford and Hethe.
1964-67	David I. Fraser
1968-78	John M. Sergeant
1978-95	Anthony Hichens (Rector of the five Southern parishes from 1983).
1993-2009	Warwick (Ricky) Yates (Rector of the Shelswell Benefice from 1995).
2009-2014	Christobel Hargraves (resigned)

Bibliography

Primary Sources

Census returns 1801-1911 (OHC).

Fringford Churchwardens' accounts (MS. DD. Fring. Par. C.1, OHC).

Fringford Parish Registers (PAR109/1/R1/3, OHC).

Fringford School logbooks (Fringford School).

Fringford School minutes (Fringford School).

The Revd John Russell Greenhill

    (a) *Diaries 1780-87* (MS.English Misc e.200, Bodleian Library))

    (b) *Diaries 1793-1800* (Misc.Wills 1/1, OHC)

The Lloyd George 'Domesday' Valuation 1910

    (a) Fringford Valuation Book, 25 November 1910 (DVX/44, OHC).

    (b) Cottisford Field Books 1912-15 (IR58 65196-7, National Archives).

    (c) Fringford Forms 37 1912-15 (DVI/34, OHC).

Oxford Diocesan Records (MS.Oxf.Dioc, OHC).

W. Potts, *List and Directory* 1897-1906 (Banburyshire Studies).

Price Family Business Ledgers 1869-1917 (Price Family/M.W.Greenwood).

Rusher's Banbury Lists and Directories 1796-1896 (Banburyshire Studies).

Trade Directories, including *Gardner, Harrods, Kelly's* and *Post Office*.

Books

E M.G.Belfield, *The Annals of the Addington Family* (1959).

J. C. Blomfield, *Deanery of Bicester, Part V, History of Fringford, Hethe,Mixbury, Newton Purcell, and Shelswell* (1890/91).

Christine Bloxham, *The World of Flora Thompson Revisited* (Tempus, 2007).

Fringford School, *Fringford Church of England School 25th Anniversary Yearbook 1972-1998* (1998).

John Gorman, *Banner Bright, An illustrated history of the banners of the British trade union movement* (Allen Lane, 1973).

Joy Grant, *Hethe-with-Adderbury,The story of a Catholic parish in Oxfordshire* (Archdiocese of Birmingham Historical Commission, 2000).

M.W.Greenwood, *Fringford Through the Ages* (Alden Press, 2000).

M.W. Greenwood, *Villages of Banburyshire,* including *Lark Rise to Candleford Green* (Wychwood Press, 2006).

M.W. Greenwood, *In Flora's Footsteps, Daily Life in Lark Rise country 1876-2009* (Wychwood Press, 2009).

Pamela Horn, *The Real Lark Rise to Candleford, Life in the Victorian Countryside* (Amberley, 2012).

Gillian Lindsay, *Flora Thompson: The Story of the 'Lark Rise' Writer* (Robert Hale, 1991).

The Rotary Club of Bicester, *The Bicester Story – Reflections of Town and Village* (The Rotary Club of Bicester, 1999).

John M. Sergeant, *A History of Fringford and Newton Purcell-cum-Shelswell* (1980s).

John M. Sergeant, *The Story of Hethe, Oxfordshire* (1980s).

Flora Thompson, *Lark Rise to Candleford* (Penguin, 1973).

The Victoria History of the Counties of England, A History of Oxfordshire, Volume vi Ploughley Hundred (1959).

Kate Tiller, *Church and Chapel in Oxfordshire 1851: the return of the census of religious worship* (Oxfordshire Record Society 55, 1987).

INDEX